SUPERVISION SECRETS – THE QUICK WAY TO EARN MORE MONEY AND MAKE YOUR LIFE EASIER

I want to thank the hundreds of people I have supervised over the years. My apologies to the ones in the beginning, before I knew what supervision really was, and my thanks to the people I supervised later on, who allowed me to discover how to really supervise.

I owe a debt of gratitude to the more than 1,000 university students who have sat through my classes. It was in these classes that we held the discussion and debate which made this book possible.

My special thanks to my sister Jean Farrell, who is a professional writer and helped me with the nuts and bolts of writing a book.

TABLE OF CONTENTS

FORWARD

Do you work in a technical capacity? Did you get your job because you have a degree in electrical engineering, accounting, chemistry, computer science, or medicine? If this technical degree qualification describes you, your income is limited by the amount of work that you as an individual can produce. If you want more resources from your work life you will need to rely on more than your individual output; you will need to harness the productivity of others. The way you accomplish that is through supervision.

Why a book about supervision? Because supervision is the most valuable workplace skill. It is valuable because getting people to do what the organization wants them to do is the basis of productivity. If you can effectively supervise people at work, you become a person who can multiply the efforts of others; and you become a valuable commodity. This means you can command more resources. It doesn't matter what industry you are in or the degree of technical knowledge that is required. Supervision can go anywhere as a valuable and portable skill. Skill in supervision is one of your best career advancing skills and you can take it anywhere work is done. Regardless of the industry you work in or the level of technical skills the workforce has, the principles of supervision are the same, and they are easy to learn and understand.

To many people supervision is simply, "being in charge" and the skill comes naturally as a person is promoted during their career. This is not true. Supervision, or more precisely, controlling the actions of people at work, is the cornerstone of productivity. The modern age in which we live is so plentiful only because of the discovery of the basic principles of supervision several thousand years ago by a group of canal builders who worked for a bunch of calendar wielding priests. At this point in your study of supervision that probably sounds fantastic, but by the time you finish reading this short book, you will understand why this happened and how it came about.

This book is different. We look at supervision for what it really is, controlling the actions of people in the workplace. It is not "Being in charge", it is not "Team Building", It is not "Creating a Family", It is not "Equity and Recognition". It is controlling the actions of others. Although this sounds harsh, it is not. It is simply setting the stage for people to be the most productive. You will find that few people in the workplace really understand how to supervise others and spend most of their time trying to follow popularized "fad" theories or simply blundering along. Understanding what supervision is and how it is applied in the workplace gives you a big advantage.

Supervision is not hard to learn. In just a few hours, you will know more than 95 percent of those without formal training who have been supervising people for years. You can begin applying this immediately in your workplace. The ability to control the actions of others at work is one of the best business skills a person can have. It will make your life easier, provide you with a path to more resources and give you a new way of looking at work.

This book will change the way you think about work and enhance your career. Regardless of whether you are an ordinary worker or a senior manager, supervision is the key to your career advancement. Supervision makes you a person who can get things done by helping others to be more productive. This multiplies your value in the workplace. Everyone, from the most basic employee to upper-level managers can benefit from this easy-to-acquire, but seldom mastered, skill. If you are a supervisor wannabe or a senior technical manager who is responsible for others, the basic skills you need are the same. They are all in this book, and these skills are easy to master.

WHY DO I WANT TO BE A SUPERVISOR?

Most people become supervisors simply because it pays more. In fact, the ability to get people to work hard to accomplish goals or get things done is one of the highest paying skills in our society. Some people consciously want to be promoted and try hard to gain recognition while others just sort of get selected somehow. But being put in a supervisory role is just the beginning.

New supervisors are often shocked to find out how difficult it is to be successful and how ambiguous the role is. As a supervisor, you are always in a state of flux and ambiguity and you are never finished supervising. For example, if you are a building contractor who builds a house, you begin with the foundation, put up the walls, etc. and eventually you are finished. When the house is done you give the owner the key, collect your final payment and you are off to your next job. You are done! Supervision is different from other work in that you are never done. You will never get to the point where you say to your workforce, "Okay, I'm finished, you are all supervised now, so I'm moving on."

As we will see, the basic principles of supervision are common to just about all areas of work. There may be some task-based differences in the amount of input and collaboration with the worker who is supervised, but overall, you supervise janitors and landscapers with the same methods and skills as you use to supervise senior managers and scientists. This makes supervision a unique and portable skill because you can take it anywhere and, no matter what you do, you can earn more if you do it supervising others. Not many supervisors know very much about it, and when you finish this book, you will know and understand more about supervision than 95% of those who are supervising others every day. This knowledge will make your life easier, make work more enjoyable and enable you to earn more money.

This book is divided into two sections. The first section concerns how to supervise people at work. The principles, such as leadership and conflict management, are universal to all supervisory jobs regardless of the company or type of work. The second section addresses the unique modifications and considerations you will need to make in order to adjust to different organizations and government regulations. Throughout this book, many points are reinforced by real life experiences of actual working supervisors or are taken from college graduate program studies of the workplace. All of the cases and examples have been highly modified to conceal the identity of the people involved. Names, locations and even occupations have been changed, but this does not alter the nature of the experience we can learn from. Once you have finished this book you will see how little most of the people who supervise understand it and how poor they are at doing it. The ability to successfully control the actions of people at work is one of the best business skills a person can have and is a powerful tool for career advancement.

WHAT IS SUPERVISION?

We all use the word supervision but few of us understand what supervision really is. As an academic study supervision is the direction and control of people at work. This is distinct from management which is the planning and control of work. It is important to recognize this difference; supervision relates to people and management relates to the tasks which people perform. Most people confuse the two, so let's look at them in detail.

SUPERVISION VS MANAGEMENT

Most people don't make a distinction between supervision and management or think they are the same thing. Supervision and management are actually very different. Supervision is the direction and control of people at work and management is the planning and control of the work process. A person can be a supervisor (direct people at work) without being a manager, and a person can be a manager (planning and control of work) without supervising anyone. In most workplace situations, many supervisors also do some management, and most managers also do some supervision. It is important to realize that supervision and management are two distinct and different activities requiring two very different skill sets.

Supervision and management within the bureaucratic framework, (the way we organize work) permeates all aspects of our lives except for our immediate family relationships. You need to realize that this is a learned, and not instinctive, behavior. The management, supervision and bureaucratic system we use was created by the Sumerians approximately 5000 years ago. It has gradually spread over the earth because it is a more efficient way of accomplishing work. Later in this book, we will learn more about this new concept, and its shady beginnings, that made our rich, modern world possible.

Interestingly enough, Americans are very good at planning and controlling work, (management), but we, as a society, are poor supervisors. If you become even an "adequate" supervisor, you will have a real edge up on other people who supervise. By the time you finish this book, you will realize that most supervisors you have met know little or nothing about how to supervise. Perhaps that is why people who can successfully get others to do things make a lot more money.

Supervision - The direction of people at work

The direction of people at work is the most difficult of all production related tasks. Supervision means constantly functioning in a state of flux and ambiguity, and few people feel satisfaction from being a supervisor. The reason this is worth mentioning is because many new supervisors feel that something is "wrong" when they are constantly faced with problems relating to their workforce. This state of flux and ambiguity is normal to supervision, and success is measured in percentages rather than absolutes. The beginning of the transition to supervisor is generally the most stressful and most difficult part of the journey, as Mark found out.

Mark worked on an assembly line, and he was a productive and well-liked worker. When the lead was promoted to area supervisor Mark was asked to move up to the lead position. As such, he was a working supervisor responsible for assigning work to his 22 other co-workers. After a few days Mark hated the new job. Rather than support him, as he had expected, his co-workers expected that he would protect them from management rules and let them do what they wanted, like long lunches, being late and not working on stuff they didn't like. Mark was mad. After a few weeks of putting off open conflict he finally exploded at Mary when he caught her turning in work that was obviously not finished.

"How can you do this?" Said Mark, "We were friends and now you stab me in the back by making my job harder!"

Mary replied, "Mark, I remember when you were one of us and took small things you needed home in your lunch box. You are supposed to help us! Don't preach to me!"

This is a typical scenario for a new supervisor, especially one who supervises people they formerly worked with. Changing roles can be difficult, and the people you expect to support you in your new role often expect you to support them instead.

Let's start with some of the basic parts of supervision and management before we get into history and theory.

All work requires coordination of effort. We accomplish this by giving workers assigned tasks, complete instructions and assigned time in which they are to accomplish these tasks. But just giving tasks and instructions is not enough. You must give clear, specific instructions on what is to be done, monitor the workers during their efforts and hold them accountable for specific results. These three elements: specific instructions on what is to be done, monitoring them periodically to make sure it is being done, and making the employee accountable for the results are the core of the supervisory process. It is the responsibility of the supervisor to do this. Workers who do not receive good instruction and direction, workers who are allowed to do work poorly without correction and workers who do not have a review of their performance have not had proper supervision, and hence have not been allowed to perform properly. The three basic principles of supervision are:

Specific Instruction

Monitor Efforts

Accountability Review

Supervisors also need to be aware of the role they play in the system. Many new supervisors see supervision as a "status reward". Just like workers, supervisors are accountable for results and represent the organization, not themselves. The supervisor's job is to make work more efficient and as such, they are a resource for the worker. This view of supervision, as the supervisor supporting the worker to make work more efficient, is the correct one.

Management - The planning and control of work

All but the simplest tasks require planning to be accomplished with the best utilization of time and resources. The basic method of controlling work is a four-step process. Work begins with a goal of what is to be done. The next step is the development of a plan to do the work in order to meet that goal. Here managers decide what segments the work will be broken into, what time it will take to do the work, what sequence things should be done in and how many resources will be needed. The third step is to monitor the plan as it is being executed to see that the work is proceeding according to the plan. The final step in the work control process is to take corrective action on those things which are deviating from the original plan.

Goal

Plan

Monitor

Correct

It is important to remember this four-step process because it is common to all work control situations. You, as a manager, may only be involved in a part of the process, but no matter what your role, knowledge of the four basic steps, Goal, Plan, Monitor and Correct is essential to your success in controlling work.

THE STUDY OF SUPERVISION

Supervision is the skill of getting people to do what your organization wants them to do. In one sentence that sounds simple, but in actual practice supervision is the area of work which has the greatest ambiguity and the least applicable principles. It would be correct to say that supervision is much more of an art than it is a science. There are few hard and fast rules upon which you can rely when faced with making a judgment.

Most of what we do in supervising others is based upon empirical knowledge of how similar actions have worked for us, or others, in the past. The best way to study supervision is to look at standard practices and formal research and then apply those to specific case studies. Throughout this book we will look at supervision in the workplace and see what we have learned in practice through reading about actual workplace cases. By studying supervision in this manner, you will not only remember the broad-based theory behind the problem solutions, but you will also experience the flux and ambiguity which is the unavoidable element of supervising people in the workplace.

The study of supervision is much like learning to play tennis. You can learn, through reading and study, all there is to know about tennis. You could memorize the weight of the tennis racket, the velocity of the ball, the viscosity of the court surface and become knowledgeable with all of the strategies used in major tennis matches. You would know just about everything there was to know about tennis. But having learned all of this, you would still not be able to hit the ball on your first day on the court. To some extent, there is a parallel in supervision. It is only through studying the cases and examples and hearing the opinions of others and then applying them to the workplace that will allow you to completely master the subject.

Supervision is much more than telling others what to do. It is also being responsible for the actions of others and responsible for getting others to do what the organization wants them to do. This is one of the most difficult elements of supervision for the new supervisor to grasp. Supervision in not being "in charge," it is being, "responsible". Responsible for giving people clear and concise directions, responsible for letting them know what the quality of their performance is and responsible for directing the work force in the manner proscribed by the organization. Supervisors don't make rules, they implement them and, at times, enforce them. And, when things don't go right, they are responsible for correcting the workplace efforts, as Eric discovers in the following case study:

Eric had been a journeyman carpenter for a framing sub contractor for five years. [these are the guys who build the wooden frames on houses and apartment buildings] During that time he had done well, and as a cooperative worker he was well liked. When the foreman retired, Eric was asked if he would like the job of carpenter foreman. With a pay increase of almost $15,000 per year Eric readily accepted.

His first project as a new supervisor was the framing of an apartment building. The work was scheduled to take eight weeks but due to running out of material, absenteeism and a long list of items that had to be corrected resulting from the city building inspection, the job took eleven weeks to complete. At the end of the work the boss called him into the office and told him that, "His performance on the project had been less than expected." Eric protested saying that there were material shortages, some absenteeism and a long list of corrective changes from the building inspector, which delayed the work.

The boss responded by letting Eric know he was responsible for all of those items; He should have signaled the office regarding the material problems before they delayed the work. It was Eric's responsibility to minimize absenteeism, and the long list of corrections from the inspector was a result of his failure to maintain a quality standard during the work.

Eric had approached supervision with the same perspective he had used as a carpenter. As a supervisor this orientation did not work. When he was a carpenter Eric was not responsible for any actions other than his own. As a supervisor, just working hard and doing it right was not enough. He had to direct the work of others and foresee the future. Eric did not understand the broader scope and the added concept of being responsible for the actions of others as part of his new role. Because he did not understand the new job requirements of supervision, he assumed that the material shortages, absenteeism and long list of corrective items were things that, "just happened" and not things that he allowed to happen or caused by not acting to prevent them.

The concept of supervisor responsibility goes beyond giving instructions to people at work: Supervisors are also responsible for the interface between employees under their direction. A supervisor is responsible for giving the employee clear and concise direction and providing the employee with feedback as to how he or she is doing in the performance of their work. This often involves a degree of conflict and can be unpleasant.

Mike was an engineering manager for a software

company. He directly supervised three programmers who were responsible for making the product. Mike created the overall work methods and software architecture, the three programmers wrote the code, and initially the project was running well. One of the programmers was very difficult to get along with. He often tried to assume authority and tell the other two programmers what to do and how to do it. Usually his comments, although undiplomatically and gruffly made, were correct.

The two other programmers complained repeatedly to Mike regarding the third. At one point, Mike tried to talk to the disruptive programmer about his interference, but he was met with an extremely hostile reaction. Eventually, the other two programmers threatened to go to the company vice president and quit if something was not done about the third. By this time, there was open animosity between the programmers and work output was suffering. Mike then terminated the third programmer for uncooperative behavior. The terminated programmer brought suit against the company for wrongful termination.

While the disruptive programmer may not have been a salvageable employee, Mike was negligent in his responsibility to both the organization and the programmer to keep the worker informed as to how he was doing. Mike had attempted on only one occasion to discuss the programmer's disruptive behavior. When he met with initial opposition he never got around to following up. Mike should have addressed the situation early and kept addressing it until there was a resolution either from changed behavior or termination.

To let the matter go unmentioned, and then suddenly terminate the employee, was not in the best interests of either the organization or the employee. It deprived both of the opportunity to settle the conflict at the lowest level of resolution by the employee simply changing behavior. Because he did not like conflict, Mike avoided it and neglected his responsibility to keep employees informed on how their efforts are measuring up to expectations. While he was excellent at planning and controlling work, Mike was a poor supervisor because he did not understand his role in that position.

Employee Expectations

Societies change and as they change the beliefs which people hold also change. In our society we can see a change in the way people view work over the last few decades. This is actually an alteration in the way we as a people demand that society treat us. To supervisors this translates into different expectations as to how they should treat subordinate employees:

Robert, an older man, was foreman on a printing crew. He had started his work career in the 1980's and had learned supervision by being supervised over the years. Now, near retirement, Robert was responsible for many younger workers who often, "refused to do what I tell them". While he gained a certain amount of respect for his age and extensive knowledge, Robert felt that the, "new breed" of worker, as he called them, was rebellious and pleasure oriented. He looked forward to retirement and getting away from supervision.

Robert supervised a young employee who was consistently sloppy in his work. Robert had several discussions with the worker and finally was at the point where he gave the young man a three-day suspension notice to "get his attention." When Robert was young, giving an apprentice a suspension would have been so humiliating the person receiving it probably would have quit rather than accept it. In this case the worker responded by saying, "Can you make it five days?" Robert complained to his boss that young people have absolutely no work ethic and that the country was headed for doom because of this.

While work ethics may have changed over the years, what Robert was really experiencing was the change in what members of society expect from the workplace. All societies are in a dynamic state of change and alteration. In our workforce we can see that younger people, in general, expect the workplace to bring them a mental and emotional satisfaction which older people do not expect from the work environment. Often, they want their work life to reflect a vaguely defined set of values or beliefs. The expectation often means that people will respond differently to similar events. In Robert's perspective the workplace provided only resources to live a satisfying life away from work. Many younger workers expect that this satisfaction should come from work itself and should also reflect or enhance specific societal values that they believe in.

Neither of these extreme perspectives is right or wrong. The workplace is based upon productivity. At least in theory we organize work and workplace behavior standards to achieve the greatest amount of work with the least amount of effort and resources. We call the effort to make something "inputs" and the product "outputs". But in order to maximize our outputs and minimize our inputs, we also need to recognize the values of the people we supervise. These differing values often require different supervision techniques.

Key Concepts

Supervision is a role and a behavior which must be learned

Supervision is a responsibility not an entitlement

Things your mother never told you

People who have never been supervisors usually have little understanding of the   supervisory role

You will undoubtedly make mistakes as a supervisor. Learn from them.

Assignment

What is the person who supervises you responsible for?

How well do you think they understand this responsibility?

Where Did Supervision Come from and Why Do we Use It?

Based upon Productivity
The concept of Role as different from the individual filling the role
Begins with the Quantification of Time
Authority, Responsibility and Accountability

We use supervision because it increases the amount of work productivity. There are many theories as to who started it and why, but for our purposes the best one to look at is the Sumerians. This may seem a little off of our topic of supervising people at work, but give it a chance. If you know how and why the role of a supervisor was created, you will better understand how to use it to your benefit.

Thousands of years ago the early Sumerians were basically a mud hut civilization which practiced sharp stick agriculture. They lived on the Tigris – Euphrates River delta and if you practice sharp stick agriculture you need really good soil. Remember, in our present day of John Deere plows and harvesters, irrigation and nitrogen fertilizer we can grow food almost anywhere. If all you have is a sharp stick, you need the best soil and very best conditions for even marginal success.

These guys planted grain and the grain needed water which was scarce in their dry climate. Here's the catch: the water came from flooding which was caused by rainfall in some distant mountains where there was a predictable spring rain. The rain swelled the rivers with water containing nice rich soil in the form of silt, which flooded the adjoining land in their valley. This provided moisture and a fresh supply of nutrient rich soil. Sounds simple: The water comes every year and floods the fields and the wheat, (or whatever it was) grows.

Now it gets a little more complicated. The rain that swelled the rivers fell so far away that the mud hut people did not know where it came from. (We now know it was mountains in current day Turkey) and here is the tricky part: You had to plant at just the right time <u>before</u> the water came. Too early or too late and the crop would die and you would end up starving. Here are the risk elements for our sharp stick farmers:

If you planted too early, the wheat sprouted and grew, and then the flood water came and washed the little plants away or drowned them. Result: You starve.

If you planted too late, the flood water came, the wheat sprouted, but it ran out of water before it matured, and the crop dried out and died before it produced any grain. Result: You starve.

So, the ideal scenario was to plant the wheat about 3 weeks before the flood; the fields get flooded on schedule, the wheat sprouts and you get a crop about eight weeks later, just as everything dries out. But, to do this, you must know when it is three weeks before the rains that you can't see, so you need to have an accurate calendar. The development of this calendar was the beginning of organized work and the mother of supervision. However, it came in a roundabout way.

Let's go back to the beginning. Imagine we are a part of this society, and basically it is loincloths, mud huts and sharp sticks. A good parallel is that you go out and live in your back yard. Your house is gone, your tool shed is gone, even your Weber bar-b-que is gone. All you have is a mud hut and a sharp stick. Sounds pretty hopeless. One or two mistakes in predicting the rain and you are out of business, by starving to death.

Now comes one of the great leaps of humanity. Someone(s) in this sharp stick culture developed a system of numerical measurement and a calendar. The number system they developed was based upon 60, rather than ours which uses a base of 10.

What's more, the evidence shows they must have understood the earth was round, not flat. At this point you are probably laughing; why 60? Did they have a lot of fingers and toes?

Maybe they did, but you will stop laughing when you realize their number system is still with us. You are wearing it on your wrist. They are the reason why our circle is 360 degrees, and the hour has 60 minutes, and a minute has 60 seconds. They also gave us the distance measurements of leagues, fathoms and nautical miles which work good with their concept of measuring time. In their system, time and distance can divide in and out of each other – try that with your number system! Their year had 360 days with 5 days left over for a big party. They had quantified time. If you lived in your back yard with no tool but a sharp stick, could you have come up with something this great? Probably not.

So, did the inventor(s) of the new calendar and number system come running out of their mud hut to tell everyone about the number system and calendar? Nope, apparently they did not. Instead, they said something to the effect of, "The Gods make the flood, and we talk to the Gods." And that was the beginning of their theocracy.

They became priests and moved into the big temple with all the food and the dancing girls while the mud hut guys continued to sharp stick the fields and plant the grain about three weeks before, the now accurately predicted, rains. This was sort of like our contemporary "Billy Sunday" salvation scams, only theirs was based upon some hard science that they kept quiet about. It is one of the first examples of basic research paying off for the researchers, and it is also the beginning of supervision. But there are still two more steps.

Our calendar-wielding priests did one additional thing. As they grew old, they did not appoint friends and family members to fill their place. They took smart kids from the community and taught them how to do the math, (and probably made them promise to keep the secret). To us this is a, "So what – we do it all of the time," but in human history this was the first major use of a "role" that a person could move in and out of and it was an <u>entirely new</u> concept.

Prior to this the power of office resided only in a person. Now things changed and the abstract concept of a "role" was born. It is not new to us, our society is full of roles: Teacher, student, supervisor, mayor, etc. Roles are in every segment of our society except immediate family life and we accept them as a natural part of the human condition. Most people are very surprised to learn that "roles", which people can move in and out of in a society, are not something which occurs naturally, they were created, and it happened about 5000 years ago, and the mud hut guys did it. This new concept of "role" is the key to understanding the big change in society that was about to come.

And now for the last step. With the new calendar the rain was predicted accurately, and the food grew, and so did the population. Soon the flooded areas were not big enough to feed the growing population. Time to build a series of dikes and canals to deliver the water to even more areas so even more people can be fed. This was a big undertaking and the community had to build a lot of dikes and canals and trenches, etc., to move the flood waters inland. This required lots of people working to build stuff. The same guys who controlled the calendar now controlled this massive public works project. They learned that if every 10 to 15 workers had someone in charge (the first supervisor!) they would get a lot more work done! And, just like in the organization of their temple hierarchy, they used the concept of "role". Supervision was a role of responsibility, accountability and authority which a person could assume (or step back out of,) and the key concept here is that <u>the role exists separately from the individual</u>. This marked the start of the modern age.

This all sounds simple to us, but it was a remarkable creation because the same amount of people now did a LOT more work simply because of the concept of role. Bureaucracy was born, and it flourished. All societies that adopted the concept of "role" function in this manner prospered. Now, 5000 years later, these societies have displaced all those societies which did not adopt the concept of role. The discovery of the concept of roles, and the supervision that goes with it, changed the human condition more than anything except the discovery of fire. The key concept is that supervision is a created role, and it is not an innate component of human behavior. It is learned and it is easy to understand.

Authority, Responsibility and Accountability

We can break down the role of a person at work into three areas. Every job has these three elements. These are Authority, Responsibility and Accountability. This is true regardless of the position in the company. To cap off our overview of supervision, we should define each of these terms:

Authority – This is the range of your control. For example, as a first line supervisor, you have the authority to assign work, review the quality of work and correct improper behavior, etc. You would not have the authority to supervise people in another department, buy major equipment or give yourself a raise.

Responsibility – An employee is responsible for a range of things. As a worker who does not supervise others, you would be responsible for doing your task(s) correctly, reporting your progress and needs and working cooperatively with others. As a supervisor, you would be additionally responsible for the work of others, including the quality, volume and timely delivery of the product or service. You could not (or should not) be responsible for those things over which you have no authority.

Accountability – If something happens, good or bad, who

is responsible for it? If your team does not get the product out in time, the organization's answer cannot be "Oh, too bad!" There has to be a person or persons whose role was to make sure that happened. If it did not happen, you are accountable for not doing what you were supposed to. Without accountability, mistakes and inefficiencies are rarely corrected.

These three elements are the key to every workplace role. Sometimes we see organizations where employees have authority for something but never get, (or manage to escape) the responsibility and accountability for their job. As a supervisor, you need to know your limits of authority, what you are responsible for achieving and what you are accountable for. You should also know these limits for each of your employees and you should be sure that they thoroughly understand them.

Key Concepts
Supervision is a "Role" which a person assumes, and the role has Authority, Responsibility and Accountability.

Roles are not natural to human nature and although very common now, were first created about 5000 years ago.

Things Your Mother Never Told You
The concept of role created the numerous benefits of modern society.

You must understand your role to be a successful supervisor.
Assignment
What is the scope of authority and range of responsibility for your job?

What are you accountable for?

ECONOMICS AND PRODUCTIVITY

Productivity Components
Inputs and Outputs

Supervision exists for only one reason, to increase productivity. Productivity is the use of time and resources to produce something. This usually comes as a surprise to many new supervisors who often think of supervision as a status reward for being a good employee. To understand supervision we need to understand the basics of productivity, which can be a very dry subject.

Sally worked on a production line. The product was carefully assembled electrical components for military use, which were tightly scheduled for delivery in conjunction with other assemblies. The work was semi-skilled and needed precise attention to detail. There were 12 other people on her line and because she was a good worker, Sally was promoted to "Lead" when the old lead retired. Since she had been working on the same assembly line for four years no one gave her any coaching or training. On Friday, she went to the old lead's retirement party and on Monday she moved to the first workbench and assumed the lead job. There were several reports on pre-prepared forms due each week and Sally had to make sure that the 12 workers had their components and instructions and were able to assemble the items. All went well for a few weeks, and Sally adapted easily to her new role.

At the end of the fourth week Jane and came to Sally and said, "I need a new unit to work on because they are still out of a part in the stockroom and I've done everything I could without it." Jane could not continue on her current unit without it, which meant the unit was stalled until the part came in. Sally checked and found out that the stock room was indeed out of a part because some had been defective and had to be returned. The stockroom was patiently waiting for the new replacements to arrive.

Sally informed her manager of the delay, and the company made an effort to expedite the replacement part. The unit was delayed by three weeks because of it.

At first glance this seems like a stock room problem, and to some extent it is. But this case also shows that there was a failure of supervision at Sally's level. Jane had known for some time that the part was not in stock, but she worked around it until she could go no further. When work stopped, she told Sally but by then there was no alternative except waiting. While it is the stockroom's responsibility to maintain and control the inventory, it is also the production supervisor's responsibility to know what is going on. Sally should have established good enough communication with the people she supervised so that they could warn her of potential problems. True, the stock room should have acted differently, but that does not absolve the supervisor of being aware of what is happening in their area of responsibility and taking corrective action before the work stops. In this case the alarm did not go off until the work stopped. Productivity was lowered because Jane did not mention the part shortage until it stopped work.

Had Sally known ahead of time the parts could have been replaced with less, or no, loss of productivity. Sally should have built the understanding and expectation with the people she supervised that potential problems must be communicated as soon as they are suspected. Making sure people kept busy was only a part of Sally's job. She had missed the part about supporting productivity because she not establish good communication with the people she supervised.

Productivity is the utilization of time and resources. The resources can be material or they can be the resource of labor which is human effort. To fully understand the role of the supervisor you need a basic understanding of the components of productivity. This is simple to grasp and helpful because it is the basis of all supervision. The best way to think of productivity is to envision all work in terms of inputs and outputs. Here are some simplified examples:

Inputs:

Material

Money and Capital Investment – such as a factory building, software, etc.

Labor

Time

Outputs:

Product

Service

Avoidance of problem

You can increase productivity in several ways:

Increase inputs to get even more (proportionately) outputs.

Biggo Construction buys all of its carpenters nail guns for $1200 each (input) and a case of speedy nails for $100 (input). They train the carpenters for four hours in use of the nail guns at $350 each (cost of training is an input). After training, each carpenter can produce 50% more output. If a carpenter can do $3000 per week worth of work without a nail gun, they can now do $4500 worth of work each week with the nail gun. Thus by increasing the inputs by $1650 per worker (nail gun, speedy nails and training), the workforce now produces $1500 a week, per worker, more in outputs. The additional inputs will pay for themselves in about 6 days and then continue, "minting money" for Biggo.

A small capital investment (nail guns) pays off big by letting each person accomplish more work. We could also consider the nail guns as a "capital investment" in process equipment. A similar situation would be the purchase of almost any automated equipment, computers, production machinery or even employee training.

Decrease inputs and get the same outputs to get more productivity

Speedy Delivery had four drivers that picked up and delivered items throughout the city. The four drivers handled an average of 20 transactions a day each for a total daily average of 80 transactions for all drivers. These 80 transactions were the outputs. The four drivers, their vehicles and gas were the inputs. Speedy changed the way in which the work was assigned. Each driver had formerly been given a stack of transaction orders and went about the work as they thought best. Speedy changed this so that pickups and/or deliveries were grouped near to each other. This made the work more efficient and they were able to do the same 80 transaction per day (output) with only three drivers and three vehicles (input).

The above example shows a change in the way we work with increased outputs accomplished by a change in the way we process information. This resulted in less travel time and allowed, in this case, the same amount of work to be done with only 75% of the inputs.

Inputs stay the same but output increases through quality control

Bill was a project manager for a drywall sub contractor. They were a large firm which did a large share of the commercial work in the market area. Each job that was competitively bid, resulted in about five percent additional labor costs for punch list items, which had to be corrected after the job was finished. Most of these involved uneven texturing of the finished surface. Over the period of one year the amount of money spent on callback labor was approximately $400,000 or five percent of a $8,000,000 direct labor payroll.

Bill decided to try to reduce this amount. He did several things to accomplish this: First, he told all of the foremen that they were responsible for completing a job with minimal callbacks. Second, each time there was a callback he had them produce a short written report as to what went wrong and why it had been missed in the initial work on site. Third, every month he reviewed these with the foremen as a group and they discussed how they could have been avoided. The callback rate fell to two percent within six months. The amount saved was approximately $120,000 per year. The $80,000 difference is attributable to more time being spent on the initial texturing.

What Bill did was to informally change the standards by which the foremen's work was measured. His organization had always stated that they wanted, "Quality work with no callbacks!" But, while they said that, they actually did nothing to make quality a measurable standard. The only thing a foreman ever heard regarding performance was, "How long did it take and how much did it cost?" This translated into the work being done as fast as possible to the "minimum quality standard needed to get by." In their hurry, the foremen's estimate of the "minimum acceptable quality" resulted in about five percent of direct payroll being spent on callbacks.

By requiring the foremen to report on the callbacks and discussing them monthly, Bill had changed the standards on which their performance was measured. Once foremen became responsible for callbacks this new attitude was transmitted to the workers who became responsible for doing it right the first time. It is important to note that Bill did not threaten the foremen with increased quality requirements nor were the monthly meetings accusatory in any way. He simply built an information exchange regarding the callbacks and by placing, for the first time, some attention on the callbacks it created a new measurable work norm (standard of behavior) which informally corrected the problem. This is a good example of increased productivity through decreased inputs by the use of quality control.

We have looked at enough examples of inputs and outputs for you to understand their use in measuring work output versus the effort it takes to get that output. There are numerous examples of both increase and decrease and economists build much more complex models with many more, and very complex, variables, so don't go bragging about your knowledge of productivity theory. This is enough to move us on to the next step where we look at how we, as supervisors, fit into making a work force productive.

Productivity Components

Most of us generally think of productivity as working harder. If a workforce is not productive the colloquial belief holds, it is because the workers are lazy and goof off or at least do not work hard enough. In the three brief examples you just read, productivity increased, but in none of the examples did the productivity increase come from the workers working harder. Unfortunately, the "workers are the root of all productivity problems" belief is all too commonly held.

Productivity is actually a combination of three elements. They are:

Capital investment

Training

Supervision

Capital Investment in Productivity

If we look at work in a broad sense these components become obvious. Since the automobile industry has been in the news over the last few decades with bankruptcy and restructuring most of us are somewhat familiar with it, making it a good point of reference from which to start. Let's look at the US auto industry from the end of World War II until about the year 2010 paying special attention to capital investment as a component of productivity.

After World War II and into the 1960's the US auto industry flourished. The cars became bigger and flashier along with the growing economy. Unions helped their members get a good sized share of the profit and --no surprise-- the politicians jumped on this bandwagon helping forge (force?) a management / labor partnership. The US auto industry was considered a model of how industry, labor and government could work together, bringing everyone a better life.

Problems began to show up in the late 1960's when Japanese imports appeared on the American market. At first the quality of the cars was marginal, but low prices and good fuel economy gave them a small market share. By the early 1970's the Japanese cars had increased in quality and a sudden gas shortage, then a big economic issue, gave them an increased market share. By the early 1980's the Japanese cars had gained a large share of the US auto market and were considered by some to be a better product than American cars. The colloquial response was that they were being built using "underpaid labor," and, therefore, the Americans could not compete fairly. By 1990 it had become common knowledge that the Japanese auto workers were by and large better off than the American workers. The cry of disbelief then changed to, "they work harder," meaning American labor was lazy. By the late 1990's many Japanese auto manufacturers had started building cars in America with American labor. They still produced an economical product with high quality standards. Each of the colloquial "reasons" for their advantage had been refuted. What was left?

What was left was the American approach to business. There are several interesting theories, one of which is applicable to our study of the relationship of capital investment to productivity:

At this time Toyota built a car with approximately nine hours of human labor. American auto manufacturers averaged about 30 hours. It is not possible that the Japanese workers went three times as fast. The difference was robotics. But don't think of robotics as something special that only the Japanese had. Robotics is available to anyone who was willing to pay for it. American auto manufacturers took a short-term approach to the manufacture of automobiles. Buying and installing robotics requires a large capital investment which will not be paid back for many years. If a business is run only on a short-term basis, long term investments, that reduce profits in the first few years, are ignored.

Capital investment in plant and process equipment is one of the key ingredients to productivity. The Japanese did not simply blunder into robotics, it was a carefully calculated investment in research and development and a decision to make long-term capital investment in plant equipment. American auto manufacturers decided to draw the capital off in profit rather than invest it in new process equipment. The result was increased profits in the short term and loss of market share and profit in the long term. This unwillingness to invest in the future is the result of short-sighted business plans. In a competitive market the short-sighted entities will usually be replaced by those that plan ahead and put capital back into the business. While capital investment is normally a management task, as opposed to a supervision task, it is important for the supervisor to recognize its role (and also their role in supporting it) within the organization.

Training as a component of productivity

Training is the familiarization of workers with processes and procedures. Most people are familiar with the tasks they are to perform. However, the benefits of increasing the capability of an individual through formalized training in their area of responsibility by cross training them to other areas is often lacking. Cross training and increased knowledge training allows workers to be more efficient, and hence, more productive at what they do. The relationship of a construction site superintendent and construction project manager is a case in point:

Fred was a project manager for a large construction company. As such, he had a great deal of interaction with the site superintendents for the same organization. Fred was responsible for keeping project records, planning and maintaining the schedule, interfacing with the architect and owner, plus all of the other typical project manager duties. The site superintendent on the other hand was responsible for quality control, short term scheduling and manpower loading on the project.

From Fred's perspective, he would create schedules and the superintendent would not follow them. This threw off his cash flow and payment calculations, and he was continually updating everything again and again. The superintendent had a similar problem. He was getting schedules which were unrealistic and did not take manpower loading into consideration. He was constantly having to change the plan the project manager was supposed to supply him with. Lots of meetings to discuss the issues produced no real improvement.

The Director of Operations solved the problem by establishing a cross training schedule. One day each week the superintendent and project manager worked together -- not to resolve issues, but to train each other in their respective jobs. The project manager became familiar with the day-to-day management of a large construction team and the superintendent became familiar with the planning of major construction projects. The requirements of the superintendent were now obvious to the project manager, and the superintendent understood how the project manager's planning needed to be modified. In short, each one now understood the others job. At the end of six months the organization had expended 26 days in training, and the problems were solved. The net result was that the project manager was able to stop wasting effort and could now run two projects instead of one, a 100% increase in productivity.

In this case, simple cross training solved the problem and doubled the efficiency of one employee. The only input was employee time and the results were dramatic. There are many opportunities for the use of training in increasing productivity and in general, the more independent judgment a job requires, the better the payoff through training.

Supervision in Productivity

Supervision is our final component of productivity. Aside from the obvious functions of direction and organization, the supervisor is also the person who provides the motivation for people to work diligently. We will look at motivation more closely in the next section, but before we do that let's look at a case where a clever supervisor used motivation to increase productivity.

Jane was the V.P. of a small manufacturing company. She was responsible for tracking and analyzing production. The work required the processing of a great deal of information and required much computer work. The people reporting to her were required to learn simple applications software, but there was a need for someone who could perform more sophisticated database management, which often involved altering the program. Jane was too busy to go to school to learn a new skill like this one, which should be delegated.

To solve the problem Jane asked one of the younger managers if he would be interested in returning to school for a few computer classes in database management. He would be reimbursed for books and tuition but there would be no compensation for his time in school. He jumped at the chance and within one year could not only modify the programs as Jane had asked, but had additionally set up a more efficient database and resource tracking program which also produced daily reports. This was an effort far beyond what had been required. The company now had a much better control of its product and inventory resulting in greater profits. The young manager was promoted and given a salary increase of $15,000 per year.

Why did the young manager put so much effort into learning how to modify and manage software? Because he had been carefully selected by Jane as a person who would be highly motivated by the opportunity for advancement. He was a few years out of school, made about $95,000 a year and was trying to support a family. To this person, advancement -- especially advancement with extra money, was important and he was easy to motivate in this manner. It is important to note that probably any employee would have gone to school and learned how to modify the database software. The exception here was the extra effort the young manager put into the job. He went far beyond the original requirements and used his own creativity and initiative. The reason was motivation. While many other people would have seen the work as just another assignment, this one saw it as an opportunity.

Key Concepts

Productivity is measured by the comparison inputs and outputs

The three elements of productivity are; Capital investment, Training and Supervision

Things your Mother Never Told You

Lots of people talk about productivity but very few understand it

Increasing productivity is the only reason supervision exists.

Assignment

What are the major inputs and outputs of the product or service you produce?

Can you recommend a change in inputs that would increase outputs?

MOTIVATION

Theories
Effort or Satisfaction

Motivation is a broad term, and it will mean different things at different times and different things to different people. People work for a reason. The first thing to come to mind is that they need resources so they can get food and clothing and shelter. And that certainly is true. Few of us who won the lottery or just inherited Uncle Bob's millions would continue showing up for our 8 to 5 gig. In a very simple sense this basic survival need is the motivation for work. But, as a supervisor, you will find that there are many ways to improve the performance of your employees by making them "want" to work and by helping them get some enjoyment, additional benefit, or satisfaction, out of it. We are going to start by looking at a few of the more common theories on workplace motivation. Motivation is a complex study and it is safe to say that nobody really knows what motivates people consistently at different times. Like all things in supervision, there is a lot of ambiguity to motivation. Despite the ambiguity, a cursory understanding of the research which has already been done will help us in our day-to-day work life.

Depending upon the company you work for and your level in the company, you will have varying opportunity to implement motivation programs. While you may not be able to give raises and promotions at will, you can always motivate by things like recognition and positive reinforcement and you will find that sometimes the motivators that cost nothing work as good or better than the ones that cost a lot. People will work harder, sometimes a lot harder, for many more reasons other than resources. Motivation usually costs very little and often has big productivity returns so it is well worth learning about.

Our first step is learning how others have viewed motivation and why, or what, they thought made people work harder. It is important to remember that motivation, like just about everything else in supervision, has a lot of differing opinions. Motivating employees has been the subject of numerous university and workplace studies, and a lot of interesting, and sometimes complex and contradictory, theories have been put forward. For our purposes it is important to realize that theories are fun to study and think about, but they are also a little like a talking to a medieval Italian prince: Nice to listen to, but you don't want to take them too seriously.

We will find that most of the major theories of motivation have some validity, and each one can give us insight into the reason people work harder. We will also find that no theory fits every situation or circumstance, and when you take a theory out of the "lab" and put it into the workplace it only works some of the time. People are complex creatures, and people at work don't always respond in the ways we expect. That's why supervision is an art and not a science. Let's take a cursory look at what others have thought about motivation and see how their thoughts may apply to our workplace.

Maslow's Hierarchy

The best place to start is with Abraham Maslow, who created what we know of today as Maslow's Hierarchy. Dr. Maslow was a psychologist and he looked at why people acted in the way that they did. While his theory contained a whole lot more than we will discuss here, a basic overview of it will give us a good starting point for studying motivation:

Maslow said that people put out effort to fulfill needs. As these needs get fulfilled, they will not work as hard to get more of what they already have enough of and will then put effort into getting the needs on the "next level". Motivation is offering the worker fulfillment that is on their "next level" of needs.

The best way to look at this is as if it were a "stack" of needs. The very bottom of the stack is the basic needs of food, shelter and clothing. You will work hard to get those if you do not have enough. But after you have a lot of food, lots of clothing and good shelter, you will not put much more effort into getting more of the same stuff. Your goals will change because you already have enough to satisfy those basic needs. Your next level of things you want, (and hence will be motivated to work hard to get) will be things like security, good employment, adequate resources, a family and property. By the time a person gets to the top of the hierarchy of needs, according to Maslow they are motivated by creativity and other things that relate mostly to how they feel about themselves. The chart below shows Maslow's theory in a very condensed form:

Self-Actualization = Morality, Creativity, Problem Solving
Esteem Needs = Self-Esteem, Respect, Achievement
Love and Belonging Needs = Friendship, Family
Safety Needs = Security, Employment, Resources
Basic Needs = Food, Water, Clothing, Shelter

This is a little esoteric for our day-to-day life as a supervisor, but there is a lot we can learn from it. A good way to understand Maslow's Hierarchy in the workplace is to make an imaginary progression of an employee through their work life:

Let's start with a young person just out of school. We can imagine our new worker as someone on the bottom of the hierarchy. They want to move out of their parents' house, buy a car and get some nice clothes. They also want to get enough money to go on dates (or dress for them) and have fun with their friends. Basically, they need money, and the best way to get money is to get a job. So, they look hard for work, and they take the best job they can find. The job is not going to be their dream job, but it is a start, and they now have an income and can fulfil the needs that drove them to look for work. They are motivated by a place to work that gives them the minimal resources they need.

Fast forward a few years, and our young worker now has an apartment, a pretty good car, a steady income and they are engaged to be married. Their wants are changing. It is time to look for a condo, save for a honeymoon and start planning for a whole new future as half of a new family. The same income that happily supported the little apartment and dating lifestyle is not going to get a two-bedroom condo with two cars and diapers. Our person now a new set of needs that make work a lot more important, because work provides money, and they need more. Just being a worker is not likely to get the quickest rewards, and at this stage in their work life, they usually begin to look for promotion. The same young employee who was happy to come to work every day and do an adequate job, is now looking for any opportunity to grow in the company because their needs have changed. Their work output increases and they start looking to take on more responsibility if they can get it. More money is a big motivator.

In a few more years they have a four bedroom house and two cars, all with monthly payments. There are also probably one or two little kids. This employee now has needs that reach far into the future. Promotion is important and so is job security. Some will look for additional education or training to get ahead or even consider an employer or career change. Employees at this stage will take on new assignments, often just for the experience, which they hope will make them more valuable to a new employer or make them more secure with the current employer. It is this group that comes in early, stays late and enrolls in night school. They actively look to their future and their needs are long-term security and long-term growth potential. Any chance for security, advancement and career growth is a big motivator at this stage.

As our worker goes into middle age, the two kids are just leaving college, the cars do not have loans on them and the house payments are now almost nothing due to the effects of inflation. Night school is just a memory and they are on the verge of a new life without children who need constant care. Work? It is still important, but for different reasons. It is a place to go and a place to interact with people. Money is still nice, but it is not everything. Our hypothetical employees' needs have changed. They have enough money, what they want now is satisfaction. Our employee is now motivated by new challenges and new experiences and not by more resources. Offering this employee new challenges will be a lot more effective than offering them more money.

Maslow's Hierarchy gives us a progression of changing needs, and hence, changing motivators. A worker evolves, and at different times in their working life will have different things that motivate them. As a supervisor, you will see this in the people whom you supervise. Their needs will change as they change, and remember, the basic theme of Maslow is the fulfillment of needs. As a need gets fulfilled its value as a continued motivator declines as the person moves on to try and fulfil the next level of need. The key is, to the extent possible, to offer them rewards that match their needs.

Applying this to the workplace as a whole can be difficult:

Ed began his career as a retail clerk and eventually built his own wholesale company. Although a self-made man with no higher education, Ed knew his success in business depended upon productivity and reliance upon those who worked for him. As the business grew, Ed was very concerned with what he termed "employee morale." Ed made sure each person was well paid, had medical coverage, participated in a 401k and that the office environment was as nice as possible. He encouraged cooperation between workers, sponsored a company softball team and made sure office furnishings and other environmental factors looked good. Ed's employees were productive, but they were not more productive than other well-run organizations in the area.

Ed hired a business consultant to tell him how to increase the productivity of the staff. He ran some initial ideas he had past the consultant, such as giving bonuses for meeting goals, making the office plusher than it was and perhaps throwing company parties. The consultant recommended not doing these things. Her reasoning was that Ed was already putting more money into the basic workplace needs than was necessary. More of needs that were already "enough" would not result in higher motivation and additional work output. The consultant recommended that Ed increase supervisor training and offer an educational reimbursement program for the employees instead.

This is Maslow applied to a group. Once the basic workplace setting is adequate, globally increasing it will not result in more work being done. As supervisors, we need to find other ways to motivate those who work for us, beyond resources and promotional opportunity.

Formal vs Humanistic

Maslow's theory is the basis for what we call "formal" management. Everything is direct and logic based. Rules and procedures are written and available (and applicable) to everyone. There is, however, another opinion on managing the workplace and it is called "humanistic" management. The best example of the several humanistic management theories is behavior modification.

Behavior Modification

While Maslow is interesting, it is easy to see that there are a lot of other dynamics going on in the workplace. There is a basic assumption to Maslow's work, and that assumption is that a person can recognize what they need and understand how to get it. In other words, people at work are rational and can make logical judgments. They see what they need and put out effort to get satisfaction of the need. We can write this as:

Effort = Satisfaction

Not all researchers think that way, and if you have worked for any time at all, you have seen instances of what appears to be irrational or self-destructive behavior by employees. This doesn't fit in with Maslow. What if people aren't rational? What if something else dictates their behavior at times? What if they just like satisfaction? This brings us to the behavioral theories of workplace motivation.

Lumping many varied studies together will help us quickly get to the elements that are important to us in the day-to-day supervision of workers. To simplify our approach, let's say that the workers, (or any of us for that matter) are not rational in most of the things we do. We are shaped by positive rewards, which we will call "satisfiers." This goes beyond Maslow's satisfaction of needs and defines a satisfier as something that "makes us feel good" and something that feels good can be as simple as praise or group acceptance. If we get a "satisfier" we will tend to repeat that activity again to get more satisfaction. This is basically behavioral modification. A person will continue to do what gets positive results and will tend not to repeat activities that result in negative results. This changes our equation to:

Satisfaction = Effort

To apply this to the workplace changes how we relate to our employees. When they do something "good," like work hard and produce a lot, we give them a satisfier. This doesn't have to be money. It can be something as simple as praise -- "You did a good job" – or it can be group recognition like a paper certificate they can tape to the wall by their desk. Some organizations give a special parking space for a month as a satisfier. People will often work very hard to keep getting things like this. When an employee does not perform properly you don't punish them. You show them where they went wrong and make sure they don't get a satisfier. They will tend not to repeat activities which do not result in receiving a satisfier. In this theory, the satisfier and the effort to get it work together creating a cycle of satisfaction – effort – satisfaction – effort and so on. Thia can be one of your most effective tools.

In application, this theory can have good results. Let's look at some examples from construction, an industry where people often have a broad range of authority, but sometimes lack the experience that should go with it:

Ben was a construction manager in charge of building a large high rise building in mid-city. The building pretty much covered the entire lot, and the staging of material and labor was critical. Ben supervised three project managers and when he went on vacation, he put one of them, Eric, "in charge" and left for three weeks in Europe. Eric was excited at the opportunity to be temporarily in charge and worked hard at the job. While Ben was gone Eric looked over the critical path schedule and noticed that work could be speeded up by shortening the schedule in some areas. He then instructed the site superintendent to bring in certain trades early.

When Ben returned from vacation, he found the site in turmoil. Trades were bumping into each other, and there were so many cars on site there was no room for material delivery. Ben took Eric aside and explained to him the intricacies of manpower loading and showed him how to run a manpower chart on the computer.

Like the sorcerer's apprentice, Eric had meddled in an area

he should not have. If Ben had acted by formal management procedures (rational employee, Maslow's Hierarchy) he would have told Eric that his performance in terms of making a major change in the work schedule was incorrect. In a sense, Ben did do this but he did it in a constructive way. Eric was not a lazy or incompetent employee. He was a young man who lacked experience but was trying to do good. Eric had made a judgment error. Ben realized that if he "chewed out" Eric he would curtail Eric's desire to exercise judgment and take initiative, two very valuable qualities in an employee. Instead, they looked at the problem together as friends and co-workers. Eric left the experience understanding manpower loading but not having had a bad experience which would prevent him from attempting to use judgment and initiative in the future.

There is a delicate balance between behavior modification and more formal methods of supervision. In the above case, the mistake was due to trying too hard rather than not trying at all. If circumstances had been different another approach using the same logic might have been in order.

Joe was foreman for an underground sub contractor. Their main work was sewer and water piping both on and off site. Joe left on vacation and Roger, an equipment operator, was put in charge. While Joe was gone Roger was responsible for the direct supervision of the crew. On one job the specifications required two feet of sand to be placed in the trench underneath the pipe. This is an excessive requirement, and Roger believed that it was specified due to the inexperience of the engineer who drew the plans. He instructed the crew to place the standard eight inches of sand bedding in the trench. This saved both excavation and sand.

When Joe returned, he found the engineer had rejected the work because there was less sand bedding than was required on the plans. When asked about it Roger replied that he had felt the plans were wrong. He also revealed that he had talked to the engineer after the rejection and tried to get him to change the specification to eight inches, which the engineer refused to do. There was also a message from the general contractor on the job asking, "When is the trench going to get covered so we can get on with the paving?"

Joe told Roger to take a small crew out to the site, pull the pipe, dig the trench deeper and replace the pipe over a two foot sand bed as required. He also told him he had three days to do it in so the job could get back on schedule. Joe's final instruction was for Roger to call the engineer and tell him the corrections to the work would begin immediately.

In the above example, Roger had clearly acted outside of his scope of authority and the motive for doing so was not clear. He should have called the engineer and at the very least received a verbal authorization before reducing the sand depth. Joe had two choices in correcting Roger's behavior. He could have had a very direct discussion regarding his lack of judgment and authority, or he could have used behavior modification. Joe chose behavior modification. He made Roger fix the work in a short time and made him call the engineer and tell him the correction would begin immediately. Both of these were "unpleasant" activities for Roger to perform. Under the theory of behavior modification, this would prevent Roger from duplicating his error because he had a bad response resulting from his actions.

Was this the best way to handle the problem? It is hard to tell, and you really needed to be in that work environment with those personalities to decide. Perhaps a better way would have been to openly discuss the matter with Roger, and do so in a positive sense, talking about how there are limits on what one should do unilaterally, why this is a problem, and then telling him to be careful of exceeding his authority in similar circumstances which may occur in the future.

Like other motivational theories, the behavioral methods

do not work under all circumstances. We, as day-to-day supervisors, need to have them ready to apply when the situation seems to warrant it. Most importantly, we need to realize that why people work, or fail to work, is poorly understood and that flexibility and awareness is our only method of achieving reasonably consistent results. We should also realize that no supervisor or manager is able to motivate all of the workers all of the time.

A Real-Life Case Study.

Up until now, we have looked at supervision a single piece at a time. In the day-to-day workplace, supervision is a part of the dynamics of productivity. Let's look at a workplace problem that needed a solution and see how the problem could be, and ultimately was, solved:

Robert is Senior Project Manager for a large international construction company. His responsibility includes all North and South American projects. The paperwork for these projects is processed centrally and handled by a staff of seven coordinators in the main office. These coordinators process all submittals, RFI's (requests' for clarification or more information), change orders and shop drawings. The work requires a specific knowledge of construction documentation, some knowledge of the construction process, and a specific knowledge of the various personalities involved in each project. A coordinator will be assigned to one or more projects and must follow the paperwork through the entire cycle from beginning to end. This includes interfacing with the architect, owner, purchasing, sub-contractors and arranging material shipping if necessary. The work requires special attention to detail and sometimes a "sixth sense" concerning others in the chain of information flow. There are six coordinators and one lead coordinator. Their ages range from 26 to 41 years. The pay rate is slightly above average for similar positions in the industry. The department is automated and everyone has computers and iPads.

Robert's problem is turnover. The average tenure is 13 months with the most senior person at two years and four months. Since the average project is over four years in duration there are sometimes several different coordinators on each project. This break in continuity seriously affects the flow of information and there have been numerous instances where the work has been affected or delay damages, (project late delivery penalty) incurred because of this. Exit interviews with quitting employees have not turned up any significant reason for leaving and comments such as, "Time to move on," or, "I need a change" are common. Few of the employees have left for better paying jobs.

Like most supervision problems, there is no "right or wrong, good or bad" answer. The case centers around people who are simply doing their job on a day-to-day basis. There are two possible methods of approaching this problem. One method is a functional solution. The functional solution would try to maintain the project information flow while coordinators changed. This functional solution would look at a mechanism allowing the retrieval of more information through a larger database and better indexing and cross referencing. To some extent, this would alleviate the problem but it would also require more inputs in the form of worker time and IT services.

The other possible solution is to act to reduce the excessive turnover rate which causes the lack of continuity on the projects. This is a supervisory or motivational approach in that the supervisor has to discover why these people were leaving and then correct the problem. The difficulty in doing this was that the pay levels and working environment were adequate or above.

The best solution would recognize both the need for a promotional ladder and a need to build better record keeping and informational retrieval system. This would involve hard data storage and cross training, plus promoting some of the coordinators so that there would be a motivational goal of career advancement to work towards. The promotional ladder solution was the approach Robert took.

Robert developed a career path that allowed project coordinators to become assistant project managers, and move into the field at more money. Once they had made the "jump" form coordinator to assistant project manager, they were on a better career path. Robert had assumed that the employees viewed the coordinator job as a dead end, and to some extent it was. By creating a career ladder, the coordinators had something to look forward to in their career development and this cut the turnover rate to about one third of what it had been. Robert still lost people, but now they went to other jobs in the organization. This kept the continuity, as they were available to train, and then continue to help, their replacement. No efforts were made at improving project data retrieval or cross training.

As with many workplace problems, the actions of the supervisor minimized the problem but never completely solved it. When the turnover dropped below a serious level, additional effort at correcting it completely ceased. This is typical of many workplace solutions.

Motivation through Values.

Most people want to be accepted as part of a group. The group can provide support but most importantly it provides a feeling of belonging and self-verification. We want to believe that our group is the "good people" who hold the right values or beliefs or whatever it is that defines the group. The less secure a person is in their own self value the more they identify with the values the group gives them. This is the basis for political movements, election outcomes and even cults over the millennia. People will follow these group values even in the face of evidence contrary to the values they espouse. As you might expect the most influenced are younger people who lack life experience.

Some organizations have used this as a motivator. The military uses patriotism or sometimes "toughness" to recruit and motivate young soldiers. In recent years a few workplace organizations have applied this to motivating their employees. Teachers are people who," dedicate their lives to children". Other organizations have espoused a green motivation to their work or a peaceful use of their product pledge. While these are good thoughts for society, they are basically a way to motivate the young people you want to work long hours at often tedious jobs. By doing what the company wants, they can become one of the "good people", and often people who are "better" than other people. It gives them a feeling of self-worth and belonging larger than the job.

Key Concepts

Motivation (and much else in supervision) has two broad theories; Formal and Humanistic

No motivational method is consistently successful

Things Your Mother Never Told You

The most effective thing you can do is to recognize an employee's good work.

Be careful to consider your organizations policies and culture when motivating workers

Assignment

Are there motivation programs where you work?

Are they "formal" or "behavioral?

ORGANIZATIONAL STRUCTURE AND GROUP DYNAMICS

Like individuals, organizations have their own culture and behavioral norms. What is "proper" behavior in one organization may be improper in another. You may have seen this difference in the organizations you are familiar with. Some are very formal and others very informal, and the same dress and behavior that is "good" at the financial investment firm would be laughable at the software development company. In some organizations the culture dictates long hours of work, but at your local government office the employees get up from their desks at five PM on the dot and leave, each and every work day. In each case, and in every combination in between our two extremes, the environment seems "correct" to the people who work there (or at least to most of them.)

One way we can conceptualize this is by looking at the X-Y Theory. It was put forth back in the 1960's by a professor at MIT named Doug McGregor. Dr. McGregor used two extremes to represent two very different types of corporate culture. This culture is based, said McGregor, on the very most basic philosophy of what people really are. We call this the X-Y theory and rather than being a continuum, it is two completely separate ways of thinking. Here, is a very shortened, and real world modified, form of what McGregor said:

X-Y Theory

Behavioral dynamics is conditioned through the reactions a person experiences as a result of their actions. We have touched upon this topic in the last section. The basis of modification through behavioral dynamics is the rewarding of good behavior. Taking this a step further, we can define working organizations as having two possible types of management. The first we will call the "X" type organization. X type organizations are run on rational rules with a strict hierarchy and well defined roles for employees at every level. In the X organization all employees are considered to be rational people capable of recognizing company values and perceiving how they can obtain rewards by following the proscribed rules and behaviors of the organization. All information, at least in theory, flows from the top down.

Levels of authority in a type X organization

The "Y" theory of work organization believes people are not rational thinkers. Y theory says that by treating people as if they were in a social organization more work will be accomplished. The key to the Y organization is the individual. In a Y structure organization the individual is seen as being essentially self-regulating and able to function without numerous rules and the strict organization of information flow, if there are sufficient social rewards for correct behavior. Do not equate the Y theory with lack of control. The difference between X and Y is the method of control. X is controlled by formal rational rules. Y is controlled by behavior modification and group norms. Both organizations use control to manage work. Both organizations use these methods in the belief that they increase productivity.

Levels of authority in a type Y organization

The methods by which a supervisor is supposed to function can differ greatly between organizations. Mike, a corporate purchasing manager who has worked in the same capacity at both types of organization, relates how the differences between X and Y appeared to him. Because his experience reveals so much of the distinction from a personal perspective, it is included here in the first person with little editing:

I began my career after getting out of school as a junior purchasing manager at what I will call the "X" company. They are a large international firm, and my job was to assist the Purchasing Manager with contract negotiation and purchasing. I worked on everything from small open PO's to new large single source contracts. We were responsible for the western part of the United States, which basically meant about nine cities on the west coast. This was my first real work experience.

The first day on the job I received a loose-leaf corporate handbook which outlined all of the "rules for X company". In the book was an organizational chart, a list of holidays, some information about the medical benefits and a whole lot of information regarding what was expected of me. As I recall now, years later, the progressive discipline procedure was outlined and there was a lot of information regarding being a "family member," and there was information on an appropriate dress code. You have to remember this was over 20 years ago when I got this first job as a kid. I remember taking that handbook home and reading it several times the first night. I felt that I had "made it" with my first real job. I was very proud. As I look back on the book, it was very well done. It really did tell you just about everything you needed to know about the organization and what was expected of you.

My boss was pretty good. He's retired now but I play golf with him a few times a year. He was probably one of the reasons why I have been successful in business. When I was a kid, he was pretty rough on me. If I didn't do something right he would pull me into his office and chew me out. Also as a manager, I was supposed to wear a "dress shirt" and tie every day. It didn't matter how dirty I got or the fact I saw only the same few people every day. The big boss [several layers up] was "Mr.," and you didn't just go see him when you wanted to. I was expected to follow the chain of command. If the bosses' boss talked to me, I was specifically not to talk about work unless asked. When I said [before] I would get chewed out, you've got to understand it wasn't like being punished. It was more like being "corrected" in a very blunt way. You got chewed out; you knew exactly what you did wrong and what you should have done, and then it was over and completely forgotten. There was never any anger in it, so you didn't take it personally. Now that I look back on those times, I can see that underneath that gruff front he was kind of laughing inside. Sort of like, "the Kid made a mistake," and it was kind of funny really.

I worked there for 19 years. By that time, I had been promoted to the Director of Purchasing for the central states, which was mostly the Midwest. I supervised, indirectly, about 70 people and we still did a combination of electronic development and manufacturing, and these were in several locations. As a supervisor, I patterned my style after my first boss, which was pretty much the style everyone used. The company handbook was bigger than when I started, but the rules were about the same. There were new chapters on avoiding discrimination and harassment, and the dress code was up to department directors rather than being universal. Employees were still warned that being late more than three times a year was grounds for termination.

When I had a problem with an employee, I chewed them out like my old boss. If I really had a problem, I used progressive discipline. Now with progressive discipline you have to know that if I didn't use it, I would not be doing what I was supposed to be. Remember, the organizational rules are for everyone, not just the lower levels. But you can also play the rules a little. We were also responsible for some things the maintenance department did. Once, a maintenance guy was supposed to put some blacktop on a parking lot. Usually, we would contract this out through facilities, but this was a small, fill the pothole, job and a maintenance supervisor had this guy pick up some cold mix in a company truck and fill the potholes. They got the cold mix using a standing purchase order with a local vendor which sort of put it under purchasing.

Well, he had some "left over" so he patched someone's driveway for $50. This all came out because one of the plant employees saw the truck and turned him in. Under the rules this was theft and grounds for immediate termination. The maintenance person had been with the company about 20 years with no problems. It seemed stupid to fire him over one small incident but I had to follow the rules like everyone else. I got the maintenance guy and the union steward in my office and told him, "I'm gonna save your butt this time, but if you do something like this again, I'll personally walk you to the door".

I wrote him up for the incident and charged him 40 cents a mile for using the truck and also recommended that he be docked for three hours of pay. I wasn't supposed to do that without running it by personnel and he also did not directly work for me. When they got the paperwork my boss, the VP of operations, asked me why I had ignored procedures and told me that man should be fired for theft. I pretended I had made a mistake and said I should have fired him, but by the time I realized it, he had already been disciplined and you can't be disciplined twice for the same incident. I got told to brush up on the rules and start following them.

By this time, I was making a lot of money, and thought I would probably stay with the company for the rest of my working life. We had three children and a comfortable life. Nice house, friends and all of that stuff. One day I got a call from a headhunter, [management placement recruiter]. He asked me if I would be interested in talking to a west coast company about a VP of Procurement job in California. I was about to say no when I thought that my present job was pretty much a dead end. In my organization there was no VP of Procurement. I was a director, and the next step on the ladder was general services VP, which was too broad in scope for me to ever be promoted into. I went to California for three interviews, and we [by "we" Mike means his wife and himself] decided to take the job. We were both from California and had never really adjusted to the Midwest winters in all these years. Also, our relatives were in California, the kids could go to good colleges for little [relatively speaking] money, and the VP job paid a lot more.

The new company I'm going to call "Y" and it was run very differently. I hadn't realized this in the interviews, so it was quite a shock to me. Let's start with the handbook. It had a few pages of the obligatory legal stuff like harassment and discrimination policy and holidays, but instead of being a "Family Member," I was now a "Team Member". There were virtually no rules in the handbook. It was mostly a listing of activities you could participate in and a vague organizational chart that showed how different products were made. Remember, except for a few part time college jobs I had never worked anywhere besides X. To me Y seemed out of control.

What are the differences? It's so different it's hard to explain. The people here are pretty much in charge of themselves. Anyone can talk to anyone about anything. If I want to go see the president, I just go hang around his office. Everyone is first name. There are no restrictions about who says what. As a supervisor, I am not a person who "controls" others; I am a person who "helps" others. It is sort of like the organizational chart was turned upside down with the worker at the top. Management "supports" the worker rather than directs them. I get rank and file workers, whom I would not have even known existed at X, coming to see me with requests and ideas. Most of the ideas are pretty bad, but some are good. If they don't like what I do [meaning the workers] they tell me how bad my decisions are. That took some getting used to.

If someone really screws up, there is no discipline unless it is malicious or grossly negligent. Then I don't write them up, I send them to counseling. There are two types of counseling, and I'm talking about the first type. At counseling, a panel of workers and supervisors hear what happened. I have to go and give my side of the story. Virtually every time the panel gets everyone to agree to work together. What is really happening is they are putting group pressure on both the supervisor and the worker to work out a solution in accordance with the goals of the organization. It is very effective. In a sense, what it does is make all conflicts a public matter and forces people to conform. The second type of counseling is voluntary if you are having an emotional problem such as a divorce or family illness. You go see an individual counselor in that case. It is more of an in-house medical benefit rather than a performance related issue and usually doesn't involve the supervisor.

The whole company is like that. While there appears to be no formal rules, there really are a lot of rules, but they are not written. For instance, if someone does good --

meaning they are performing well-- I am expected to reward them with positive feedback in some manner. This does not mean money. It means telling them, and everyone who will listen, that they have done a good job. You always want to reinforce proper behavior and actions. If a person makes a suggestion, you need to reinforce the fact they made a suggestion regardless of its value. If a worker comes up and tells you that you made a bum decision the first thing you do is thank them for letting you know how the decision affected their work. Then you explain why you made it and ask for some alternative suggestions, if they have any. Nobody told me any of this. When I first started working here, I chewed someone out and ended up in counseling for "yelling at them." I was mad then but it's funny now.

How does this work? Having worked both ways, I think each way has its plusses and minuses. Here [meaning Y] I do less of what I would call work and spend more time talking to employees. Much of what I used to do in terms of management is done by lower levels. I spend a lot of my time talking to people and helping them make the decisions I used to make [at X]. It works up the line too. I participate in areas I never would have when I was at X. At X I just did purchasing. Here I have input into many other areas that are beyond standard purchasing. Of course, I'm a VP here and I was a director at X so that is some of it, but regardless, everyone has much broader input. Overall, both organizations make money in the same type of business. I can wear a Tee shirt to work. Big deal. Sometimes I would like a few rules to follow which were written down. On the other hand, there is less stress involved in supervision here because I don't supervise, I help the group. By group I mean the whole company. It's not without conflict either. You have to conform to this way of working. You are not nearly as independent as in X. Earlier, I told you the story about the maintenance guy who did the bandit blacktop job at X because I wanted to bring it up again. At X, I manipulated the rules to prevent him from being fired. Here, [at Y] the incident would have gone before a committee of management and workers. The committee would have most likely fired him over my recommendation. I would not have been able to prevent it. Even though they only recommend it, it's pretty much the only thing you can do.

I feel as if I'm a part of this company, but I also felt I was part of the other one. I'd say you must act differently, but really work is work, and that's pretty much the same. I've been here nine years. I like it.

Small Group Dynamics

Most people enjoy the company of other people. In the above example, we see how the Y organization used group dynamics to control the work force. They accomplished this by making most all decisions and actions open to group input and by rewarding correct (from the organization's perspective) behavior. For them, this was effective.

In the workplace, we find informal groups of people who have something in common. These groups are often outside of the formal organizational groupings. Group dynamics is the study of the methods by which people interact in groups and, of special interest to us, how groups form values (called norms) that enforce those values and keep group members in conformity.

As supervisors, we are very concerned with informal groups and the standards of behavior they create. Many of us will supervise work forces with informal groups that have formed their own unique value systems. Most of these informal group value systems limit themselves to simple interactive behavior norms. Sometimes you will find small groups, which also use their group dynamics to form, or modify, the standards of work. We can help to create group norms that are beneficial to the workplace:

Becky worked for a company that made electric power control equipment. Customers bought a package that included switching equipment, software and ongoing technical support. These customers were municipal utility districts and major users of electricity, such as automobile manufacturing plants, in various countries. She was recently promoted, and now supervised five engineers who were responsible for the software and who also provided telephone technical support to customers throughout the world. Many of the callers seeking assistance with problems were not native English speakers and could be difficult to communicate with. Customers usually called for assistance only when things were going very wrong, and they were under a lot of stress.

The problem Becky faced was the calls for assistance often went, "less than well" with the caller and the engineers becoming angry at each other. The callers' issues were almost always ultimately resolved, but they often went away unhappy, and the company had received many complaints about the "miserable support" they provided. One of Becky's jobs as the units' new supervisor was to, "fix this."

The former supervisor had sent the engineers to training on dealing with difficult customers and gave them coaching on telephone technique, but it had not worked. Becky decided to try to control the work group's norm as a way to solve the problem. The first thing she did was to acknowledge the difficulty in handling these calls. She recognized that it was very difficult to deal with upset people who often did not really understand the software, or their problem and, to make it even more difficult, could not communicate well in English.

The next thing Becky did was to hold a meeting each week where she and the five engineers talked about the calls.

But these meetings were different; they didn't talk about how they solved the problem, they talked about the callers as individuals. At first, the programmers were angry with the callers. As they told their stories, Becky was careful not to blame the engineers for not handling the calls well. They simply talked about their frustrations. Becky acknowledged their frustrations and angry feelings. By the third week, the stories were the same but the attitude had changed. They were starting to laugh at some of the things the callers said and did and even some of their own responses. The breakthrough came at the sixth meeting, when one of the engineers said, "I couldn't wait to get here and tell you all this story!" and then launched into a tale of a plant manager whom he had spent three hours with on the phone, and how he finally solved the problem by using a translator on his cell phone. The group loved this story and were very supportive of the engineer who had shown so much patience and been so resourceful.

What had happened? Becky had created a new group norm by simply letting the people communicate their frustrations and accepting them as a group. A bad call had changed from a frustrating and upsetting event into an opportunity for positive group recognition. Becky had accomplished in a few weeks what her predecessor had been unable to do in years of coaching and training. And she did it with eight half-hour meetings.

Sometimes a group's effort to force conformity can be counter-productive as we see in the following case study abridged from a doctoral thesis on workplace norms:

Case study, The Model Makers

....The [company] built machinery for drilling rigs and offshore oil exploration vessels. The model shop consisted of eight highly skilled machinists who reported to the factory manager. Their job was to make prototype fittings for test and analysis before a fitting would be placed into manufacture. The job required a high level of skill, the ability to use CNC and manual milling and cutting machines and required a great deal of abstract conceptualization and knowledge. Although model makers are not formally educated as such, it takes many years to become one, and they have a sophisticated understanding of metal working and manufacturing. They are "blue collar" workers, but are paid on par with mechanical engineers.

The eight model makers range in age from 29 to 56. They have been employed with the company from 3 to 18 years. Generally, the group functions under minimal supervision, and each model maker normally works directly with one or more engineers in creating specific prototype parts. The model makers consider themselves to be a unique group and feel they are essential to the well-being of the organization. They are proud of their skills. The group, except for one, gets along well with each other and they often socialize outside of work. They eat lunch together, help one another with technical problems, and are generally supportive. One of the model makers, Klaus has difficulty working with the others. The reason for this is somewhat obscure. Klaus has been with the organization for five years and at some point during this time fell out of favor with his seven coworkers. The incident(s) are not specifically mentioned, but it is obvious in studying the group interactions that Klaus rarely receives assistance from the others.

They talk to him, they will respond to his requests for information, but only minimally. Klaus never gets the same level of assistance, and he is never told things that it might be beneficial for him to know. In other words, no information is volunteered to Klaus by the other model makers. More critically, Klaus is never proactively told things. These could be items of gossip, or they could be information regarding work, or the status of equipment and schedules. There is a busy informal information communication network in most work organizations, and much valuable information flows through it. Klaus is not a part of this network, and his work suffers because of it.

The model makers group has built an informal norm limiting the information that flows to Klaus, and he often has trouble because of this. He will not be informed when material he is waiting for has arrived; he won't be told when machines are losing tolerance, and new software changes must be learned alone with no help from those who already know how. Of the eight machinists, Klaus is the least productive and the one most likely to make mistakes. The withholding of information by the group was the reason for his lower productivity.....

This problem is typical of those that supervisors face. There are no clear causes, and the problem is difficult to observe and define. We don't know why the other model makers did not like Klaus, but we can make a reasonable guess. Most likely, he had done one or more things in the past that the model makers felt was contrary to their interests as a group. Typically, this will be something like "snitching" to the boss when a fellow employee does something wrong or makes a mistake. There are two reasons why an employee "turns in" a member if their workgroup. The first, is because they have seen or learned about something important which needs to be addressed. This is correct behavior on the part of the employee.

The second reason is more subjective. Sometimes a member of a work group will give a supervisor a multitude of information on things other group members are doing wrong or incorrectly because they want to curry favor with the supervisor. Normally, the reports are on minor or largely inconsequential happenings and are done only out of self-interest. These workers are usually ostracized by the group. Klaus was probably one of the latter and had likely tried to curry favor with the plant manager by reporting minor incidents regarding his co-workers. When this was discovered, Klaus was ostracized by the group. It is important to understand that this is a "primate" reaction to a group problem, and the group members may not be consciously --or may be only partially-- aware of what they are doing. Since this is not specified in the study, we will have to assume that the reason for Klaus being partially ostracized is unknown.

Analysis of "The Model Makers"

As supervisors, we are concerned with situations like this because the group productivity is suffering. As is typical the problem is difficult to diagnose and solve. It is subtle and there is no apparent reason for it and no obvious solution. If we put ourselves in the role of the plant manager who supervises the group, how can we address this problem?

The model makers work under minimal supervision. The plant manager is listed as their supervisor on the organizational chart, but in reality he only "stops by" a few times a week to see how they are doing, or more frequently if there is a problem. As highly skilled and mature workers, they do not need to be constantly observed or monitored, and even though the plant manager is their supervisor, most of their assignments and work interactions come directly from the engineering department. Requests for material and supplies are generally made by the individual model makers or the engineering department and are routinely signed off without more than cursory scrutiny by the plant manager.

Closer supervision would allow better group interaction with Klaus. While not openly hostile, they are acting in a way detrimental to the organization. If Klaus was in fact a "snitch," it should have been nipped in the bud by the plant manager.

By listening to, and reacting to, what is essentially gossip level communication the plant manager would be partly at fault for Klaus' lower productivity. At this point, there is probably no quick solution. Klaus' productivity is still adequate even though he is the least productive worker in the group. One course of action is to hold a brief meeting with the group several times a week to discuss work and schedules. These may help bring Klaus back into the fold. Klaus' input should be solicited in the meetings, but the plant manager should be careful to look for behavior on Klaus' part which would set him apart from the group. The meetings should focus on the group as a work unit that does things together, and any goals for the group should be addressed as a group effort. The model makers need to be reminded that it is their job to support one another.

The plant manager might also try to find out why Klaus is ostracized. One way to do this would be to wait for a specific instance when Klaus was not told something, and then simply ask why he was not told. Normally, under these circumstance, the answer would be, "I don't know" or, "we forgot" but it would be a good opportunity to mention that everyone needs to support each other for the group to do well, and they should be sure to keep Klaus "in the loop." If Klaus is really a person the group considers to be unwelcome, the passive resistance will continue. If the cause of being ostracized is based on only one or two instances, this will probably work.

The plant manager needs to be careful to address the problem only in terms of "working together" and "productivity," and should avoid any reference to personality. Finally, if the problem gets worse, the plant manager will need to become more direct and address the problem as a specific performance issue with one or more of the model makers. This means using progressive discipline or counseling, which will be covered in another section.

The "Team" as Group Norm Control

Over the length of your career, you will see the rise and fall of many popular supervision theories. They are usually incorrectly named "management theories" and as I write this, (2023) the current popular theory is "Teams". Everybody is part of a team, and you help the team accomplish results. I can remember several "amazing new ways to manage a workforce" over the last few decades. They usually start as popularized books that spark a trend. There is nothing wrong with the concept of "Teams". But as a supervisor you need to see teams for what it really is, the control of people at work through the control of group norms.

As your career progresses you will see "Teams" fade and a new "best way" replace it. It is important to realize they these are cycles of change like fashion styles and not cycles of improvement. The latest method is not better than the former ones. As a supervisor you need to go along with your organization when they adopt one of these as the gospel or if you have a supervisor who believes they have discovered the latest secret to getting people to do things. But in reality, it is nothing more than an attempt at controlling workplace group norms.

Key Concepts

All organizations control worker behavior. Some emphasize formal and direct control, some emphasize group behavioral control. Most use a combination of both methods

Group norms are rarely understood by supervisors.

Things your mother never told you.

Be careful to understand and conform to the dynamics of your organization.

Recognize that group dynamics can be one of your best career enhancement tools

Assignment

What are the control dynamics in your organization?

How could you improve the dynamics of the group you are part of at work?

LEADERSHIP

We can say a person is in a "position of leadership" for two reasons. First, they can be in a position of leadership because they are placed in that position by the formal organization of the company. Second, they can be in a position of leadership because they are recognized, by members of the group, as being able to benefit the group, and have accepted that recognition. This distinction between an organizational position of leadership, and the leadership which exists because the group informally creates or acknowledges a leader, is an important one to supervisors.

As we have seen, behavioral norms in the work group can be an important element in productivity and very critical in the supervisor's role. This brings us to the area of leadership. You will hear a lot about "leadership;" Things like "the 25 traits of successful leaders" or "how to be an effective leader" or "leading difficult people" are popular sample topics as this is written. They all promise to give you everything you need to be an effective leader, without putting a whole lot of effort into it. Leadership is the most difficult part of supervision, but it is also the area that yields the greatest results.

Let's review the rationale behind supervision. Supervisors exist only to increase productivity. The role of a supervisor is one of responsibility, and not a role of entitlement. Supporting people at work involves making sure that they have the resources, material and knowledge they need to do the work and involves controlling their actions at work. In other words, to some extent, the supervisor decides what they will do. This directing of the workers' efforts is the area where leadership is important.

Leadership is effectively making the group believe you are helping them to accomplish their goals or fulfil their desires. Look at the examples of leadership we see in our everyday lives. When we elect a politician to office, we are really selecting a leader, a normal primate function for humans. We look for people who we think will help us in some way or ways. That help may be in increasing our economic well-being, or making sure certain rights are available in our society or improving business conditions in your down town area. The more serious politicians hire consultants and do studies to try and find out what the "voters" want, and then try and tell us what we want to hear, (hopefully within limits) so we will vote for them. In its rawest sense, this is leadership. At work, we can look at it more simply as supporting the group in achieving the group's goals. It's important to remember that, unlike politics, the organization sets these group goals and not the people in the group.

As we have just seen in the model makers' case study, workers often have a great deal of leeway in the way they behave at work. If we can control or influence the group dynamics of our work force, we have become a leader. The best way to begin our study of leadership is to look at what others have done in the past to try and understand it. Like most things in supervision, there is not "one answer", some things work some of the time, and nothing works all of the time.

A good place to start is with the military. They are very concerned with leadership, because they need to control group dynamics if they are to win. If you look back at history, you will see many examples of people like Alexander the Great and Genghis Khan, who consistently defeated much larger armies mostly because of good leadership. It is often the quality of leadership, and not resources or numbers that wins battles and makes nations successful in conflicts. The military is a good study because it is an organization that gets people to do things not only that are not fun things to do but could also get you maimed or killed.

In general, the military sees two ways to lead; You can "Demand" or "Command." They see the best way as co-manding with to "CO" part meaning that the leader and the group work together as partners to accomplish a common goal. Remember the Sumerians a few chapters back? They were the first people to formalize the leadership role, and they did it to improve productivity. The leader existed only to make the group function better and this is the best view as far as productivity is concerned.

Leadership is not always letting the people being lead participate in the task. Neither are good leaders necessarily "liked" by those who are led. One way of looking at leadership is to generalize and look at leadership as having three possible styles. While very simplistic, doing so helps us to start thinking about what leadership is. The three basic styles are:

Authoritarian – This style of leadership places all decisions and authority with the supervisor. They may, or may not, solicit input and feedback from the supervised. Basically, they decide what needs to be done, tell the workers to do it, and there is strict control over the workers. This is the typical "old time" boss, and roles are very structured, and communication is one way, from the top down.

Democratic – The democratic style leader makes decisions, and sometimes policy, a "group" effort. Not only is the input of workers solicited, but they also have some say in the decision making process. For this style to work, it requires strict control over the process to keep inside the bounds of what the organization requires of the worker. Communication is two way and individual contributions to the group are encouraged and expected.

Laissez-Faire - Leave them alone or "hands off." The leader delegates tasks and then lets the worker make the decision, offering guidance and assistance when requested.

The leader sets the goals, but the rest is up to the workers, with little or no direction, unless guidance is specifically needed or requested.

Keeping in mind that the above styles of leadership are much too generalized to be helpful in real life, let's look at them applied to a specific situation. By doing this we can see how each style works in terms of getting the job done, so that we can better understand the relationship of leadership style to work output. Because the military has done a lot of work on leadership style, let's use a make-believe military example:

You are an army lieutenant in charge of a platoon of 30 battle-hardened soldiers. It's the declining days of World War Two and you are in northern France fighting against a better trained and well-equipped German army. Right now, it is dawn and you are at the bottom of a hill looking up across the steep fields in front of you. About 800 yards away, on top of that hill, is a walled monastery full of German soldiers who are starting to shoot at your platoon as you huddle behind what little cover you can find. Your job? Go up the hill, and take the monastery from the Germans by Noon, suffering as few casualties as possible. You are the leader and it's time to get started. First, you need to give the group the goal:

"Okay guys, Listen up!" Our job is to take that monastery from the Germans, and we have five hours to do it. That's right, it's the big stone building in front of us, the one with all the Germans inside who are shooting the bullets and cannon shells at us."

Now let's apply each of the three leadership styles to your task and see what you say next:

Laissez-Faire ....."That's our job men! Go to it!" I'll be here in case you need any help!"

Democratic ...... "Okay guys, let's get together for a few minutes and decide how we can best do this. If we have a lot of different opinions, we can hold an informal vote."

Authoritarian ...... "We will move up the hill in two squads. One fires at the enemy to keep their heads down while the other moves forward in leapfrog progression. Fifty yards each move. Squads ready! On my count! Squad one is first on three! One, two, three...."

In this scenario, authoritarian leadership would work the best, and the other styles would work poorly or may not work at all. It is important that we realize that our leadership style must be flexible and will need to change with the task and with the skill and maturity of the workers being supervised.

Our interest is in the type of leadership which will be most productive. It is obvious that being given a "position of leadership" by the organization does not mean the supervisor will be able to lead. To effectively lead a work force, the supervisor must match the style of leadership to the task at hand and make the group believe that he or she benefits the group in achieving its goals or, at the very least, is not detrimental to them.

Ken worked for several years for a concrete sub contractor. When his boss retired, Ken was promoted to foreman. He now supervised the same people he had worked with as a co-worker. Like most new supervisors, he tried to be a "friend" and supervisor at the same time. He believed a person should be able to work with little direction and felt reluctant to criticize the crew or to exert any authority because of this. He gave them broad assignments, made sure they had what they needed to do their work, and then left them alone. This went on for several weeks until Ken noticed that the work was getting sloppier and the productivity lower. One morning, before work started, he told the crew that they would have to pick up the pace and stop being so sloppy. Ken began closely monitoring their work and giving them constant instructions and surveillance.

This resulted in no improvement, and again Ken told the crew the quality of their work and the output had to increase. The response had been much the same as it had been when he left them alone. They told him he was power mad, and they felt betrayed.

In the above case, Ken had used the two extremes of leadership. At first, he essentially delegated all work and had little or no interaction with the workers while the task was underway. When that didn't work, he went to the other end of the spectrum, and began telling them how to do their jobs step by step. The second approach was no more effective than the first. Not surprisingly, the crew had the same low productivity response to each approach. They also did not seem to make a distinction between Ken's two styles of leadership.

Although Ken had the technical knowledge and experience to manage the work, he was not accepted as a leader by the group. He had a "position of leadership," according to the company organizational chart, but as far as group acceptance or recognition of his leadership, there was none.

Ken's problem was that he was not matching his leadership to the task. At first, he delegated all decisions to the employees with poor results. The second attempt at leadership delegated nothing and ken was essentially constantly telling them what to do. Neither method worked.

Situational Leadership

Some of the best research on leadership has resulted in the concept of "situational leadership." This theory matches the style of leadership to the task that needs to be accomplished. This is one of the best theories of leadership, and it was developed by two guys named Paul Hersey and Ken Blanchard. They said (in short form) that the style of leadership must be matched to the task AND the amount of involvement and skill which the worker contributes to the task. Hersey and Blanchard's theory went way beyond the simple, and highly modified, version we are going to use here, and they are well worth reading for additional information.

The "involvement" contributed by the worker in doing the task is the horizontal axis of the following chart and the "task definition" is shown on the vertical axis. Involvement is the amount of the creative use of judgment by the worker, and task definition is the degree to which the work is defined. This gives us two variables, the amount interface with others needed to do the work shown on the horizontal axis and how much independent decision the worker must make which is shown on the vertical axis.

Task Definition -----→ HIGH Low ←-----	Participating **2** Well defined task & a lot of judgment	Selling **3** Well defined task and little Judgment
	Delegating **1** Poorly defined task and lot of judgment	Telling **4** Poorly defined task and little judgment

HIGH <-------------Job Task Involvement ----------> LOW

The table above combines both involvement and task definition and shows how the style of leadership relates to the changes in these to variables. As these two elements change, the best type of leadership for the job also changes. While this may sound complicated, keep in mind that it is basically a simple theory, and there is no rocket science involved here. It is just a way of matching worker control styles to job requirements to get the highest productivity. There are two variables: the amount of independent decision making the employee must do, (called Task Involvement) and the amount of dependent interaction, (called Task Definition) with others, that the job requires.

Let's begin by looking at each segment of the table as if we were studying an automobile manufacturing company called Detroit Motors.

Square 1 Delegating - The President of Detroit Motors is basically told by the board of directors to "go make money." He oversees the entire operation and makes all the necessary decisions. This includes selecting designs, setting manufacturing levels, setting sales prices and a host of other activities, most of which are accomplished through others. Nobody checks to make sure he comes to work each day. He doesn't need approval to do things and most importantly he does not need to keep in contact with the board of directors to do the assigned tasks. This job has Low Task Definition in that what you need to do on a day-to-day basis is not well defined. The Task Involvement for this job is high because the president must make most of the decisions on how the work is done. From a supervision standpoint, this job is best supervised by telling them what to do and then letting them do it. Low involvement from the supervisor (in this case the Board of Directors) with this position will get the highest level of productivity.

Square 2 Participating – The General Manager of the Detroit Motors manufacturing plant is in charge of making the cars. He reports to the President. The General Manager makes sure the cars get made, and he must coordinate the design, tooling, material and labor needed to produce the cars. He must coordinate his efforts with the design and marketing departments and keep in touch with the President. This job has High Task Definition in that, what must be done on a day-to-day basis is very well defined and involves others. The job also has High Task Involvement because the worker must make many independent judgments on a day to day basis. The best style of leadership for this task is Participating, and our General Manager is constantly in touch with the President and other company managers, both giving his input and getting input from others. From a supervision standpoint, this job is best supervised by working closely with the employee as a partner and making sure they have the information flow and cooperation they need to do the work.

Square 3 Selling – After the cars are made someone has to sell them, and that job falls to the car salesperson. Our car salesperson must show the cars to the potential buyers and convince them to buy the cars. They also sell add-on items like alarm systems, extended warranties, and undercoating. The Task Definition for the salesperson is high. What they must do on a day-to-day basis is well defined and requires a good deal of interaction with others in the organization. However, the amount of Job Task Involvement (judgment) is Low. Basically, the task is, "sell cars for the price we tell you". There is little for our salesperson to decide, use initiative for, or plan on their own. They do not set prices, they do not control inventory, and they don't have a lot of input into creating the work that needs to be done. They simply, "do it" within proscribed limits. The best way to supervise jobs such as this is to keep them informed of things like price, features and availability, which they need to know to sell the cars. They should be given sales figures and sales goals and kept motivated by the supervisor. Without supervisory contact assuring the flow of information and providing feedback on performance, productivity will fall.

Square 4 Telling – The cars sitting on the sales lot get dirty and dusty. The cars aren't going to sell well if they don't look good, so the person with the "car detailer" job must go look at them every day and dust them off or wash them to make sure they are clean and good looking for the prospective customers. This same person also cleans up the incoming cars as they come in from the factory, pulls off the protective plastic covers, vacuums them out and makes sure the interiors are clean. The task is basically, "clean the cars" and it is not very complex, nor does it require a great deal of dependent interaction with others. The job also takes little involvement and therefore requires little in the way of judgment. Basically, the only important decision our car detailer gets to make is whether or not they are going to come in to work that day. This job has both Low Task Definition and Low Job Involvement, and the best style of supervision is telling the employee what to do and then reviewing their performance periodically. Little involvement is needed to keep the job productive.

Before we move on, it's important to note that most people who study this theory of leadership initially start classifying all supervision jobs as a "1" or a "3", etc. Don't do that! The chart is really meant to display a generalized continuum of possibles. The amount of each variable changes by job, and the whole thing is only a tool to help you conceptualize leadership in a somewhat structured way. Like all theories in supervision, it has something to teach us, but it does not work all of the time. Note also that different employees, at different times in their career, may move around on the chart. New employees and beginning workers need a lot more task involvement by their supervisors than an employee who has been doing the same job for years. Use it as a tool to help you think about leadership but realize that the four squares are snapshots on a continuum of possibles and, like all theories; you should take only what works for you from it.

Let's look at a few examples of situational leadership in action in the real world:

Bob was site superintendent. The firm he worked for hired a new construction manager to whom Bob now reported. For the first few weeks, the construction manager spent quite a bit of time with Bob learning the field operation and getting familiar with Bob's project, which was a large one. Bob had been with the company several years.

Things went well during the familiarization period,

but by the time three months had passed, problems were developing. From Bob's perspective, the new construction manager was very unhappy with him. He was constantly changing the things Bob did. He did not like the short-term schedules and would tell Bob how he wanted them changed. He thought the site manpower loading should be different and asked to have that changed also. There were numerous other examples.

Finally, Bob went to the main office to see him. "If you aren't happy with my work," said Bob, "just fire me and get it over with. This nitpicking me to death isn't doing any of us any good." The construction manager was genuinely surprised. "I'm not unhappy with you," he replied. "I think you are doing an excellent job and I've learned a lot working with you! What makes you think I don't like your work?"

"Because" Bob replied, "you are always changing everything I do. I do a short-term schedule; you tell me to change it. I do my manpower loading; you tell me to change it. I send in a report, you ask me how come I said this and that. I put some pressure on a sub, and you tell me it would be better to do it another way. I feel like all my authority and judgment is gone. If I'm responsible for what happens out there, then I need to be able to do it, not do it once and then do it different for you."

Although neither Bob nor his boss was able to articulate the problem, the issue was supervision. Bob, as site superintendent, was responsible for the day-to-day operation of the site. He made many decisions and exercised a great deal of judgment. His job was not well defined and required a great deal of employee involvement. The construction manager was supervising Bob as if his job had less of an independent judgment requirement. The construction manager fluctuated between "telling" and "selling" in his style. What was required was the participation style of leadership. The construction manager should have participated in decisions and procedures with Bob, but not taken the judgment away by changing what Bob was doing, without thoroughly discussing it with him and reaching a mutual agreement.

Note that neither of the parties was aware that the problems they experienced were caused by using the wrong leadership style. Bob thought his new boss was trying to pressure him into quitting. This is typical of instances where the supervisory style is inappropriate for the task. The person supervised often decides the supervisor is trying to make them quit or doesn't care about them. In reality, the problem is the style of leadership.

As supervisors, we need to be aware of the leadership style required of us and also of our subordinates whom we supervise. Much of how we lead comes from the examples of how we have been lead in the past. It is often difficult to make the transition from one method of leadership to another unless you consciously analyze the task and judgment required of the worker. The concept of learning from a role model is an important one. Not only do you learn from those who have supervised you, you also are the role model for people that work for you. In any organization, subordinates have the tendency to adopt the leadership style of their supervisor and reflect that style on down the line. This can cause problems:

Joan was V.P. of United States product development. She supervised Ed, who was a product director and had responsibility for developing several complex products. Because his work required a great deal of judgment, Joan worked closely with Ed, but the decisions he made were his, not hers. Ed supervised a large staff of engineers and scientists which also included a clerical unit that directly reported to him. While his work in relation to the engineering development and research functions of his job was excellent, the clerical support department he was responsible for was a disaster. They were constantly creating ways of doing things that did not match the rest of the organization. They produced reports in formats no one was familiar with, they messed up the bookkeeping, and they even changed computer software to a "better one" at a cost of $180,000 before they realized it couldn't interact with the home office system in Europe.

The problem was Ed's style of leadership. He supervised everyone with the same style of leadership Joan used with him. This high task definition style worked well with the engineering and research employees he supervised but it did not work at all with the clerical staff. Even though they were mature, intelligent people, their overall view of the organization, and the amount which their tasks could be varied was very limited by the nature of those tasks; therefore, the judgments they were allowed to make were usually wrong. Ed should have used the "Telling" style of leadership to keep them within the parameters of their tasks. Joan, who was also responsible for the group, should have made sure Ed was supervising properly.

Employee vs. Job Centered Leadership

Do not confuse this with the X-Y theory or with Situational leadership. Job centered supervision orients all supervision towards the needs of the organization. Employee centered supervision is based upon the belief that employees who are satisfied or happy with their working life will be much more productive. This increase in productivity will occur regardless of the problems which may be encountered by orienting much of the supervisory effort towards keeping people happy. In an abstract sense, both job centered and employee centered orientations are designed to increase productivity. The first works by controlling employees to create productivity, and the second, by creating worker satisfaction to increase productivity. The bottom-line objective is productivity with both theories.

The basis of employee centered supervision is employee involvement in organizing the tasks they are to preform and allowing them some level of decision regarding how work is to be done. This is common in many organizations. In most cases, employees who perform a task requiring an average or higher level of involvement will perform much better if they have some input into their working lives. For tasks that are very well defined, the involvement of employees in decision making generally lowers productivity rather than increases it. This theory of employee versus job centered supervision, although not applicable to all positions in all industries, is relevant to most jobs. Employees often have a great deal to contribute to the work being done, and letting them assist in planning and executing the work will make them more satisfied and hence more productive. Studies have shown that an orientation at either end of the spectrum results in lower productivity. Sometimes the recognition of employees in decision making is a simple matter:

> John was a carpenter supervisor. At the beginning of each new project John would gather the crew together with the plans and discuss how they were going to approach the work. The crew would collectively discuss the project and collectively discuss how to approach the work and then decide who would do which tasks and how long they thought the work would take. Each Monday after lunch he would spend about 10 minutes with the crew reviewing the work and how they thought it was going. If an employee made a good suggestion, John would implement it. If an employee made a suggestion that was not beneficial, but was also not detrimental, John implemented it. His crew was the most productive in the company.

By spending a few minutes involving employees in decision making, John was able to greatly increase their satisfaction with the work. When they performed a task they felt, to some extent, they were performing their task and not one directed by the organization. In reality, the employees made few suggestions which were not obvious to John before consulting with them. Most of the organizing of the work was really just common sense. By involving the workers, the amount of effort they put into the work was increased. It should be noted that John was always careful to keep the decisions within the range of the task, which was carpentry work.

Coaching

It is the responsibility of a supervisor to help the people they supervise succeed. This is really a statement which summarizes the supervisor's role. It is your job to make sure the people who work for you have the tools and knowledge that they need to do the job. Sometimes you will need to go back up the chain of command to get these for your workers, and sometimes you can help the worker get them for themselves. Coaching is working with an employee to help them understand and perform their job better. We want the people we supervise to take as much ownership of their work as is possible and we want them to apply independent thought and initiative to the work, where appropriate. Too often new supervisors try to forcefully correct behavior when really, they should be taking a few moments to help the employee understand what is required of them, and why it is needed. This is focusing on success and works well with employees who really want to succeed at their tasks, which is most of them. By doing this you are working together to make the employees more productive.

Key Concepts

You must match leadership style to the task and the amount of judgment it requires.

Do not think about leadership in too simplistic terms.

Things Your Mother Never Told You

Leadership is not the same as popularity. Don't do things just to get people to like you.

Being given a position of leadership is not the same thing as being a leader.

Assignment

What generalized style of leadership does your boss use with you?

Does the organization you work in have a "preferred" leadership style?

STYLE

In our review of supervision, we have seen many differing opinions regarding how to lead people at work and control their efforts. As mentioned at the beginning of this book, there is little in supervision which is not open to discussion and debate. Many of the theories contradict one another, and as we have seen, no theory is universally applicable. We have studied them because they all have some value sometimes, but none have value all of the time. We, as working supervisors, now understand the range of possibilities and need to pick and choose, to the best of our judgment, as situations vary.

Each of us will apply what we have learned with our own style and personality. This is to be expected. A style which works for one supervisor may not be successful for another supervisor. As mentioned earlier, the control of people at work is the control of a dynamic system, and as such, it is an exercise in flux and ambiguity. There are, however, a few basic principles of behavior which are beneficial to all supervisors regardless of their personal style, orientation or type of worker being supervised:

1 *State instructions clearly* – Communication is a topic as broad as supervision. The most important element in getting an idea across is not in what you say, but in establishing two-way communication. Stating instructions clearly means getting the message out AND getting the message back in terms of a specific confirming response.

2 *Encourage questions* – Supervision is a two-way street and requires the supervisor to interact with the worker. The main mechanism by which a worker interacts is to bring the

supervisor information in the form of questions. Never be too busy to respond. Failure to respond or being "annoyed" tends to reduce the questions which are your most important path of information.

3 Explain the reason for rules and policies – Just putting forth the organization's rules and policies is not enough. A supervisor needs to explain them to the employee and keep him or her informed of the reasoning behind them.

4 Begin suggestions with a tentative approach – This is a method of involving the employee in the process of reaching a conclusion together. Begin suggestions, especially those of a corrective nature, with a tentative approach. For example, instead of telling the backhoe operator, "You screwed up that ditch" a better approach would be to say, "Don't you think that ditch is a little crooked?" and then continue the conversation focused upon the ditch, not the employee. This allows people to keep some degree of dignity and become involved in solving the problem.

5 Encourage the communication of problems – No one likes to hear about problems, but problems are your most common source of upward information flow. You, as a supervisor, need to know what is happening and what is not happening. This information usually arrives as a "problem".

6 Keep workers informed – How is the company doing? What are long-term goals? What are the short-term plans? You are the source of information for those who work for you. You have an obligation to keep them informed of the good, and the bad, things which occur.

7 Do not punish people – No one in any organization, regardless of supervision style, punishes workers. You may use corrective discipline or counseling to correct behaviors, but a supervisor never punishes. Treat all people equally regardless of whether you like them or hate them.

8 Set examples – You are the most prominent role model for the people who work for you. If you have high expectations for yourself, you will get the same from them.

9 Give feedback – Every employee whom you supervise should always know exactly how they are doing and never have to wait for the annual review or guess at how their work is being received. Employees have a right to know what the organization's expectations of their performance are and how well their performance meets those expectations.

10 Be consistent – Consistency means predictability. Your employees require a consistent supervisor to respond to. A supervisor who is emotional one day and calm the next is worse than one who is emotional all the time.

11 Treat people with respect – The job of supervisor is a level of responsibility, not a social status. Supervisors are in no way "better" or "worse" than the people they supervise.

12 Follow up – Do not make promises which you cannot keep. If you start something, finish it.

13 Don't make snap decisions. This is the most common sign of an inexperienced or incompetent supervisor. Supervisors often feel pressured and become emotionally involved in work situations. This leads to "snap" decisions which show poor judgment. Take time and think before you act.

14 Do not lie – A person who lies quickly loses all credibility with those above and below them. It is always better to be wrong and admit it than it is to be wrong and lie about it.

Key Concepts

How you behave towards others is very important.

Communication is very important.

Things Your Mother Never Told You

Being honest and consistent is better than being smart.

Don't make decisions too quickly.

Assignment

What qualities of style does your supervisor have?

MEASUREMENT AND STANDARDS

Case Study – What you measure is what you get.

How we measure work and the standards for performance to a great extent determines what it is we get in terms of performance. When we look at productivity in a broad sense we talk about inputs and outputs. In most industries we have standard quantitative terms for outputs such as "units shipped," "new accounts," and "dollar volume," that help us measure what it is we produce. We can say shipped 1500 computers last week, or the salespeople signed up 230 new accounts last year, or we billed for $6,000,000 in January. But, when we try to apply measurement standards to managers and supervisors, the problem becomes more complex. For purposes of simplification, we will assume that the following case is a software development problem and not an integration issue:

Lenny was project manager for Speedy Software company. They developed software for clients that needed to connect information across multiple platforms. For example, a company might have one accounting software, another software that keeps inventory, a third that controls manufacturing and a fourth used by the sales force to track customers and sales. Lenny supervised a group of programmers that made software which tied all this together. Using Lenny's software a person could sit at one screen, with one program, and run sales reports, check on inventory and send work requests to manufacturing, with all elements interacting. Most of the work was negotiated bid, and while Lenny's jobs were profitable, they also had an average of twice as many customer "callbacks" as the industry standard, because of major bugs or inconsistencies. These callbacks were always responded to quickly and the problem fixed.

Most of their work was negotiated bid, and too many callbacks for things that did not work right cost the customer money. Having to return frequently and fix problems could also mean the customer would perceive a quality and value difference between suppliers, in addition to a price difference, which could affect repeat business.

The VP told Lenny to, "Reduce the number of callbacks over the next year." Lenny gathered his programmers together for a meeting and told them, "Our call back rate is too high, and we have to cut it down substantially within one year!" They all agreed to work hard to reduce callbacks.

At the end of the next series of product releases, the rate of callbacks remained as high as it had been.

Just telling the programmers to "reduce callbacks" produced no change. The rate of product bugs remained high. The problem was measurement standards. Lenny, like most project managers, had measured the performance of his people by money and time. A good job was one that was on time and below budget. A bad job was over budget and / or took too long. By telling the managers to "reduce call backs," Lenny had given instructions but had done nothing to create a new standard. He continued to measure by the standards of money and time. If Lenny had wanted to reduce callbacks, he would have to create some sort of callback rate measurement standard and include it in his expectations for performance.

This example brings us to an interesting point. The company did a great deal of negotiated price work with repeat customers. Price was never the total consideration in a customer selecting the company as successful bidder. It is easy for a manager to assign quantitative values to time and money. It is a little more difficult to create a measurement standard for callbacks, which can be measured by frequency and staff time. But, what about customer satisfaction, how do we measure that?

A year later Lenny was back in his boss's office. "I just talked with Meggo Industries," said the boss, "and they told me they gave the factory software job to Biggo Software. When I asked why, they said we were low bidder, but Biggo was easier to deal with and they had fewer problems after the work was over. You've got to get your people to reduce callbacks!"

Lenny again called the programmers together and told them to reduce callbacks and work more closely with the customer during the projects:

"Biggo Software just beat us out on the Meggo job. We were even low bidder and that wasn't enough. Meggo went with Biggo and did it because they said we were difficult to deal with and our software had too many call backs. I told you guys to get the call back rate down and nothing happened. Now, we really need to get the call back rate down and make our customers happier with us.

The failure of Lenny to recognize two qualitative work measurements, customer satisfaction and workmanship, had finally impacted his organization in a measurable way. One of their prime customers accepted a higher bid from a competitor because the competitor was "easier to deal with" and "had fewer problems" with the completed project. They had lost whatever the profit would have been on the job because their measurement standards addressed only time and money. By using time and money as the standard by which the programmers were evaluated, the product they produced was the minimum quality needed to "get by," built fast and economically. While this instance had shown them one unhappy customer, how many other instances never surfaced?

The customers perceived Speedy Software as difficult to deal with and producing a product with a lot of defects. Lenny's programmers fought tooth and nail for every dollar in every way. Why? Because their bonuses, pay and promotions were tied to the two standards of, "how much did it cost?" and "how long did it take?" To customers like Meggo, the problem wasn't related to software cost. If they dealt with Speedy, they had to suffer from the downtime and wasted staff time that resulted from software glitches. The cost of this to customer Meggo greatly exceeded the difference in price between Speedy and their competitor.

Lenny developed the following plan:

1) The amount of call backs was recorded by job and severity, and each programmer and project manager were given a monthly report on them. Callbacks more than the average resulted in reduced bonuses. Callback totals below the average resulted in increased bonuses.

2) A separate line item of one-half of one percent was established in each project budget for "customer needs." This money was used for doing additional things, such as pre-release testing or re-writing problem areas that would help increase quality. This gave the programmers some leeway in fine tuning the project before it went to the customer without being negatively evaluated because of budget over runs.

While this system may not work for all industries or products, it does show how one supervisor met the challenge of measuring qualitative standards. It is difficult to measure callbacks by a method other than their number and almost impossible to measure satisfaction. But as long as Lenny didn't even recognize these standards, no one was going to attempt to meet them. When Lenny first talked to the programmers, he just gave increased quality lip service, but did nothing to implement it. When Meggo revealed another software contractor had gotten a job for more money the point finally sunk home. By tying the number and severity of call backs to a supervisor's attention and the amount of a programmer's bonus, the quality of work received immediate attention.

Note that there is a tradeoff between cost of the product and increasing product quality and customer satisfaction. It cost money to do the things that made Speedy Software easy to deal with, and it took more time to make sure things were done right. These were additional inputs into creating the product. This extra input resulted in additional, but not fully quantifiable, outputs of reduced callbacks and increased customer satisfaction.

We should not leave the subject of standards and measurement without discussing the application of negative standards, or those standards which work against the interests of the organization. There are three common areas of negative standard measurement and evaluation that are often detrimental to the work process:

Housekeeping – An inexperienced supervisor who is not familiar with qualitative inputs will often count "housekeeping" or "neatness" as a performance standard. This is normally done because they have no idea of how to really measure the employees' output. Housekeeping should be a standard only as it relates to safety or productivity.

Personality – They key to a successful standards program is to measure standards only as they relate to job performance. Personality is important only to the extent that it affects work and the ability to cooperate with others in the workplace. Too often inexperienced supervisors will equate how well they like, or dislike, an employee to how well that employee is performing. The same holds true for age, religion and ethnic or national backgrounds. A person should be evaluated_upon what they do and how well they do it. Do not confuse this with employees that are disruptive or have difficulty working with other employees or customers. These are job requirements for almost all positions and are an important part of any employee evaluation standard.

Error based upon initiative – The use of judgment and initiative is one of the best assets you can find in a subordinate employee. No one will be right all the time. It is better to have a person who tries and makes an occasional mistake among many successes, than it is to have a person who never tries at all. Some supervisors make the mistake of punishing, or negatively reacting to, the use of initiative when the result is not favorable. By doing this, they create a negative standard which will cause the employee to avoid making decisions.

You see attempts by businesses to measure customer satisfaction with things like customer surveys after the event. Typically, this is done by businesses like auto repair shops associated with dealerships, and medical care providers. It has become so common that, the service techs now ask you for a "5" rating before you leave. A few days after getting your car repaired a surveyor calls you for a brief survey. A national healthcare organization sends paper surveys to a randomly selected percentage of patients with the same 1 to 5 rating scale.

One of the problems both organizations have run into in some areas of the country is the ethnicity of responders based upon the language they are most comfortable using. Foreign-born customers in the US who feel they have received "Good" (what they expected) service will rate the repair service or physician as a "3" for Good, just like the caller or the form says. A native-born customer tends to rate the exact same transaction as a "5" or Excellent, if they get the service they expected. In some urban parts of the western United States, foreign-born populations can run about 30% of total. Having a lot of foreign born customers or patients who select their physician or service rep because of language, could lower the overall rating. This led to those car service reps and physicians, who were fluent in the common immigrant languages, pretending that they were only fluent in English so they would not get too many foreign-born customers and thus lower their performance evaluation. Supervisors should be aware that the metrics of measuring customer satisfaction often have many unexpected surprises.

Key Concepts

We often talk about achieving goals but have no measurement standards for them.

Once you have a measurement create a standard for it.

Things Your Mother Never Told You

What you measure is what you get.

Don't make senseless things a standard.

Assignment

What is measured on your job?

Is there anything else that should be measured?

CONFLICT

As a supervisor part of your job requirement is to enter into conflict resolution situations on behalf of your employer. Conflict is a normal and healthy part of life. The key to conflict is to understand that conflict will continually occur, and people must learn to deal with conflict and to resolve it on the lowest level. The first step in this process is to realize that conflict should not be avoided. Avoiding conflict by ignoring conflict situations or smoothing them over will generally result in a larger degree of conflict occurring later on. Read the following case where a lab manager (Ed) and project manager (Jim) both report (and complain) to the pharmaceutical manager (Bob):

Ed was a lab manager. He worked closely with Jim, the project manager for the drugs they were developing. Jim, according to Ed, was constantly telling him how to run the lab and how to prepare for drug tests and trials. Jim would give their mutual boss Bob, the pharmaceutical manager, detailed explanations on how he thought Ed should run the lab and how tests and trials should be handled.

On several occasions lab manager Ed brought this up with project manager Jim, and reminded him that as lab manager, the day-to-day operation of the testing and trials was his responsibility. Jim's response was to tell Ed that "I'm ultimately responsible for selling what happens here, so I will decide how it is done!"

Jim would agree in principle that Ed was in charge of

the lab and testing and trials, but he continued to meddle and kept telling their boss Bob how things should "really" be done in there. On several occasions, he changed Ed's schedules for testing to, "help with the manpower loading and speed things up."

After one of a series of heated arguments, Ed finally went to their boss Bob and complained that project manager Jim was meddling in his area. Bob replied that he would look into it. Ed stressed that, as manager of the laboratory, he needed to have control if he was going to get work done, and that Jim's actions were interfering with the organization's ability to get the job done. Several weeks later, the situation had not improved, and Ed again reminded their boss that Jim's interference needed to be stopped.

When a period of time passed with no change, Ed began to retaliate against Jim. He withheld testing schedule update information from Jim. He changed clinical trial protocol without telling him, and he told Jim that certain items of work, which actually were included in the trials, should be negotiated with the customer as changes. After about a month of this, Jim came raging into the lab. "Why are you doing this!" he screamed. Ed calmly replied that if Jim could play lab manager, then he could play project manager.

Jim immediately went to see Bob the pharmaceutical manager and complained that Ed was meddling in his area........

In the above example, two managers fell into conflict, probably due to the ambitions of Jim, the project manager. Ed, the lab manager, tried to settle it at a low level by talking to Jim, and when that did not work, he went to see their boss Bob. The boss listened to him but did nothing. The pharmaceutical manager was a conflict avoider. By not taking any action, hoping the issue would be resolved by itself, he allowed the conflict to grow larger. The net result was an escalation of the conflict and open warfare between two managers. This unchecked conflict affected productivity, and then caused even more conflict coming into the pharmaceutical manager's office. His non-action accomplished nothing, and made the problem grow to gigantic proportions.

Conflict often means angry people and angry people, can be difficult to deal with. Remember that managing conflict between employees is part of your job, and you need to keep in mind that you represent the company, and not yourself. Keeping the resolution focused on productivity is the first step. If an employee exhibits "bad" or "rude" behavior, you need to stop that behavior and let them know that what they did is having a negative impact on the work being done. In the following case, a supervisor addresses a conflict as a performance problem, and he does it right away as soon as it is observed.

Sam was foreman for a crew of laborers. Two of them, Joe and Fred, were required to work together. One day Sam heard Fred yelling at Joe regarding Joe's heaping of lumber in a sloppy pile. Sam went up to both men and asked them why all the yelling was going on. Fred started to tell him how sloppy Joe was and how the sloppiness made the job harder to do. Sam stopped him in the middle of his complaint:

"Look guys," said Sam, "I need to tell you both something. You are expected to conduct yourselves in a professional manner at work. That means solving your differences in a calm and rational way. That does not mean yelling at one another."

"If we are to function out here, we must all get along, and that is expected of each of you. That means piling the lumber so it is easy to pull out. That also means treating each other with respect. You are both good at what you do, but right now your behavior is not appropriate, and it must stop, and it must not happen again."

In the above example, Sam addressed the conflict immediately, and he addressed it as a performance, rather than a personality, problem. Note that Sam did not take sides or try to evaluate which party was right or which party was wrong. He did not accuse anyone of being rude or of exhibiting bad behavior (although Fred did both.) In mediating conflicts, supervisors will often find that one or both parties to a conflict attempts to get the supervisor to side with them, much as children would with a parent. They want to win, and the supervisor's agreement with their actions or anger is important to validate the victory they desire. You should not take sides in a conflict other than to discuss the proper or desired work procedure. The best method is to focus on the fact that conflict is improper workplace behavior because it affects productivity.

Not all conflict is noisy and obvious. Sometimes it is quiet and subtle, as the following case shows. Conflict is usually based upon the perception of a loss or an obstruction. If that perception can be overcome, the conflict will be resolved:

Jane was project manager for a large firm. One of the construction managers, Bill, had worked for her for several years. He was competent and did his work well. Over a period of time Jane noticed that Bill seemed to be initiating less and less contact with her. Many of his reports or questions, which used to be made informally by stopping by her office, now came in writing. She felt she was not getting the information she should be. Jane directly asked Bill if anything was wrong. "No, everything is fine," Bill replied. Jane pursued the matter and explained that she felt Bill was growing a little distant and avoiding contact with her, and that the contact was important to both of them being successful on the job. Bill responded that he felt Jane was giving all of the complex projects to the other project managers, and he was being given the less important work.

The reply surprised Jane, and she asked him what made him feel that way. Bill related several instances of projects he wanted to do, mostly bridge work, which he had never done before, but he kept getting put on freeway retaining walls (freeway retaining walls are massive, complex projects.) Jane explained that she had not realized that he wanted to work on bridges. She added that she purposely gave him the retaining walls because he was so good at them and was considered the best project manager for retaining wall projects in the firm. She told Bill that she would gladly consider him for the next small bridge project. The relationship returned to normal.

Had Jane not pursued the issue, the silent conflict between her and Bill would most likely have grown in proportion. By addressing the problem early, she was able to seek a solution at the lowest level of resolution. In this case, Bill felt Jane was obstructing his career and had created an imaginary scenario where she was purposely trying to keep him from advancing. Although Bill may have hinted that he wanted to manage other projects, he never made a direct request. Jane had no idea that he perceived an obstruction until she managed to pull the information from him. Once she corrected his perception of obstruction, the incident was forgotten.

Negotiating Employee Behavior Change

An employee is an asset to your company. They have the knowledge and skills you need in order to keep the business running. Sometimes, we do not care for these human assets as well as we should. For example: If you bought a new truck for your business, you would change the oil and balance the tires, add water to the radiator, etc. You do those things because it makes economic sense for you to do so. If you did not change the oil, the engine would blow up at about 25,000 miles and the truck would be useless. If you do change the oil, the same truck will probably run over 200,000 miles for just a few dollars' worth of oil and a few hours of time spent getting the oil changed. This is just plain common sense, and everyone knows it. So why are we writing about it? Because many supervisors do not give their employees the same "maintenance", they would give a company truck. This is an economic mistake. Your employee is a company asset and should be treated as such.

As a supervisor, you will occasionally need to modify or correct the workplace behavior of your employees. There is a systematic method of doing this called, "progressive discipline," which escalates the attempts at correcting work behavior in stages. Progressive discipline is a staged response to inappropriate or insufficient performance. How should you interact with the employee when telling them to behave differently? As a general reminder, discipline is never punishment. The supervisor acts only on behalf of the organization with the sole goal of getting the employee to behave correctly. Once the behavior is corrected, the incident is forgotten, unless the problem occurs again.

Employees have a right to know when they are doing something wrong and should be given a chance to correct it if possible. This process often begins with a conversation between the supervisor and the employee. This is stage one of progressive discipline and is called the "informal warning". About 90% of all workplace behavior problems are resolved at this level, so, it is important that a supervisor understand the process and how to manage the interaction, so that the outcome is positive for both the company and the employee. The key to success is to remain focused on workplace issues, and not be deflected into discussing other issues. In many corrective discussions, the employee will try to change the topic from the actual behavior under discussion to something else. This is called "deflection" and many people unconsciously (or consciously) do this when faced with criticism. The best way to show this is by example. We will use the simple example of an employee (Fred) who is habitually late. When Fred tries to deflect the conversation from his behavior (being late) to something else, the comments will be *in italics*.

> **Supervisor**: "Hi Fred, I noticed you were 20 minutes late today. This is happening a lot, and when you are late the people who are assigned to work with you have to wait until you arrive to get started. We need you to be on time and here by 8AM every day."

> **Fred**: "Yeah Boss – I'm sorry about that, but *I have to get my kid ready for school every day and that takes a lot of time*"

Note that Fred is changing the topic from being on time, to getting kids ready. While he probably does have to get his child ready in the morning, that is not the workplace behavior under discussion and the supervisor should not become involved in talking about it.

> **Supervisor:** That can be hard to do but right now we are talking about getting to work on time. You need to make whatever plans and arrangements you must in your personal life to be here when you should be.

Note that the Supervisor did not discuss the issues of getting the child ready and off to school. If that had become the topic of discussion, the supervisor would end up talking about how difficult it was for Fred to get there in the morning.

> **Fred:** "Well what can I do, "*With the traffic and all, I can't depend on getting anywhere on time.*"

Note that Fred tries to deflect the topic again, this time from being late to how bad and unpredictable the traffic is.

> **Supervisor:** "We all know the traffic can be bad, but you still need to be here on time. If you can't make it here consistently, for whatever reason, the company requires that I move on to the next step, which is a formal warning to be here on time. We'll review your attendance in 30 days and see how it went.

Mark a meeting on your calendar for May 15th, at 10 AM, which is one month from today."

The supervisor ends the conversation without discussing any of the deflection attempts and has stated five things clearly:

what is wrong
why it is wrong
what the correct behavior is
what will happen if it is not corrected
when (specifically) they will review the situation again.

We have used being late as an example, but in practice the same formula will be useful for just about every workplace behavior change you need to accomplish. You have probably noticed that deflection from the topic is a reaction or strategy used by many people who face criticism, and, if you have raised teenagers, you are probably very familiar with it.

Competent, but does not work well with others.

Have you ever worked with a person who was good at their job but had trouble getting along with coworkers or customers? Many supervisors make the mistake of not recognizing cooperative behavior as a part of job requirements. See the following example:

Mary was a new supervisor in a mid-sized company, and another worker had just come in and resigned. It was the third in six months, and all gave the same reason:

"I can't stand working with Shirley," said Jane. She is constantly telling me what I did wrong, and she is just plain nasty. You can't control her, and I'm leaving."

Now Mary was going to have to hire and train yet another person, but before she had the chance to put in a hire request to personnel, her boss came to see her.

"What's going on in your department? Jane just

stopped in to say good-bye, and she said she was leaving because of poor working conditions. Jane is the third one in the last few months, what's happening? "

"I don't really know," replied Mary. "She wasn't happy with Shirley and Shirley can be hard to work with, but she is excellent at her job. She is a good worker who does everything on time and never makes mistakes. People should be able to get along with her!"

Mary and her boss reviewed the last evaluation for Shirley. It gave her good marks on all categories and noted her high productivity. Neither the evaluation format, nor the evaluation specific goals, mentioned anything about getting along or cooperating with others.

"Fix this! Said the boss, we can't keep losing good people like Jane!"

According to the company evaluation and goal setting paperwork, Shirley was an excellent employee. In actual practice, Shirley was a troublemaking bully, who disrupted the department and also did a good job at individual work assignments. Mary was making the same mistake many supervisors make, and was rating employees only on specific task performance, and ignoring other aspects of workplace productivity. So how should supervisor Mary handle a problem like this?

Mary's company only recognizes and measures "output" or the amount of and/or completeness of the work which employees are assigned. This view of the workplace is too narrow. Work is accomplished by cooperation between people and people working towards a common goal. A troublemaking or disruptive employee like Shirley can be productive when performing simple or rote tasks, but the disruption they cause lowers the effectiveness of the entire workforce. When coworkers begin to withhold information from Shirley or retaliate against her, the productivity of the workplace suffers. When employees resign because of the behavior of other employees, the organization has just lost an asset and a new person must be located, hired and trained.

Mary is in a difficult position. She works for a company that does not recognize cooperative behavior as a work requirement, and does not evaluate performance in that area. Because of that, Shirley, who does a lot of work, has high marks on her evaluations. However, the same company wants Mary to, "Fix this!" and stop the high employee turnover caused by Shirley's behavior. What should Mary do?

The first step would be for Mary to sit down with her boss and explain what she thinks is causing the turnover and then ask her boss for assistance in fixing the problem. Mary has to hold Shirley accountable for her bad behavior and help her to correct it, but in order to do that, the organization has to recognize that cooperative behavior is part of the workplace requirement, let the employees know that cooperative behavior is part of the job requirement, and then measure, evaluate and reward for it. Without that support, Mary has little in her supervisory tool kit she can use to change Shirley's disruptive actions.

If Mary can get the support of her boss, she would sit down and informally talk with Shirley. The conversation should focus on Shirley's interaction with coworkers. Mary would explain that bickering employees hurt productivity and that all employees are responsible for interacting in a polite, cooperative and positive manner. She should expect a hostile reaction and denial from Shirley during this session because workplace bullies often receive a great deal of personal and psychological gratification from their actions and will not want to alter their behavior. The session should end with Shirley understanding, or at least hearing, that a new way of relating to coworkers is required from now on. Mary should make sure her boss knows this conversation is going to happen; Mary should document what she said, and also Shirley's reactions to her comments and then give her boss a briefing after the session is concluded.

It is likely that Mary will need to carefully monitor Shirley's behavior and will probably have to call her attention to several instances of improper interaction in the coming days and weeks. It is important that Mary bring these to Shirley's attention immediately to show that the new rules are "real" and to let Shirley know what, specifically, the organization will not tolerate. In time, Shirley may correct her behavior, and if she does, as with all progressive discipline, the discipline ceases when the behavior is corrected, and the employee is never punished.

Our bullying case was concerned with clerical workers in an office environment but can occur in just about any workplace setting. It is very common in the construction trades, where productivity is especially affected, and it is one of the most difficult behavioral problems for the supervisor to correct.

As a supervisor, there will be many instances of conflict in your daily work life. It is your job to deal with conflict on behalf of your employer, and to do so in a calm and rational way. Never think of conflict or resolving conflict as a punishment. It is simply a normal part of the workplace, which you must deal with on behalf of your employer. New supervisors often personalize conflict, which makes them avoid it. Do not do that! Address it quickly and early, and most conflict situations will be easily resolved.

Note that in the above case there were some new variables: The organization's policy was important because it is the "organization" that acts, and not the supervisor. If the company has no standard for cooperative behavior, it is difficult for Mary to suddenly create and enforce one. Mary's supervisor is also clueless to the need for creating and enforcing a culture of cooperative behavior. The boss just wants Mary to, "Fix this" and ignores the fact that doing so would mean suddenly introducing a new rule on behalf of the organization, a task which they do not have the authority to do. Mary really has two problems, modifying Shirley's behavior, after first modifying the company policy on cooperation. This makes her task much more difficult and shows us two things: How little her supervisor knows about supervision, and how many supervisory problems become very complex with the introduction of other variables. This is part of the flux and ambiguity that is a normal part of being a supervisor, and is what makes supervision an art, rather than a science.

The next section of this book deals with the organization, and how the supervisor relates to that organization. We will look at how the organization creates standards, relates to government agencies and laws, and how the supervisor is involved in all of this.

Key Concepts

Entering into conflict situations is part of a supervisor's responsibility.

Never avoid conflict.

Things Your Mother Never Told You

Don't personalize workplace conflict

Don't be afraid to tell employees that they are expected to work cooperatively with coworkers.

Assignment

How is conflict handled by the person who supervises you?

Does your organization have a policy for cooperative behavior?

SECTION TWO – THE ORGANIZATION

As a supervisor you represent the company. Just about everything you do or say, is done or said on behalf of the organization you work for. When you give instructions, those instructions are on behalf of the organization. When you motivate a work group, that motivation is done on behalf of the organization. It is sometimes difficult to remember this in the press of day-to-day responsibilities, but it is important to realize that just about everything you do, you do on behalf of the entity for which you work. It is important for you to understand the basics of how the role of the supervisor meshes with the dictates and responsibilities of the organization. In this section, we will focus on the way supervision integrates into the organization, and how the supervisor relates to various laws governing employment.

JOB DESCRIPTION AND JOB SPECIFICATION

A job description describes the work to be done and a job specification describes the person most likely to be able to do that job. Each employee has a role to fill, and most companies formally define that role. The first step in hiring a person is to determine what the company needs to have done. The way they do this is to create a job description, which lists all the duties and responsibilities for the position. Here is a sample job description:

Position: Bookkeeper II

Responsibilities:

Reporting to the Controller, this position records and maintains business financial records and financial transactions and keeps accounts current.

Duties:

Develops systems for tracking transactions.
Maintains accounts.
Maintain general ledger.
Prepare financial reports.
Comply with Federal and State Laws and Practices.
Work with others on the accounting team.
May supervise accounting clerks.

Required Skills:

Data entry
Peachtree Accounting Program
Turbo Tax
Attention to detail.
Able to write reports and meet deadlines.
Work well with others
Interface with customers in a positive manner
Must be able to lift 25 pounds on occasion.
Other duties as assigned.

Benefits:

Salary Range 4, $60,000 to $72,000 annually in five steps
Three weeks PTO annually (Personal Time Off)
401(k)
Fully paid family medical

Once we have the job description and know what it is we need to have done, we can then build a profile of the hypothetical person who would be most likely to be able to do that job. The job description is very definite, but the job specification is less so. It is our best guess as to what a successful candidate will look like. If we are lucky, we will find that person. You need to keep in mind that the job specification is only a guess, and it may not really identify the best candidate. Too many supervisors (and personnel departments) try to match the job specification literally to the applicants. This is often counterproductive. Here is a job specification for our Bookkeeper II job description:

Bookkeeper II Job Specification

Experience: At least two years with major accounting programs for a mid to large sized organization which includes responsibility for full ledger and reports

Required Knowledge:
Bookkeeping practices

Basic office procedure
Accounting principles

Required Skills:
Full ledger
Monthly closing
Preparing reports
Peachtree and Turbo Tax
Successful history of meeting deadlines

Education: AA or AS degree in accounting or bookkeeping or a four-year degree in related field. Experience may be substituted for education.

When you see a job listing on the internet, it is normally a combination of the job description and job specification. The goal is to tell prospective applicants enough about the job so they will make a good decision as to whether they match it, so that only good applicants will apply.

Usually, this process of creating a written description of the job, and then a specification to profile an ideal candidate works pretty well. As a supervisor, you may be asked to contribute to the job description and the job specification, and these are important contributions for you to make. You will also have a role in selecting candidates to be interviewed and making recommendations as to who should be hired and who should not be considered.

There are a few pitfalls that can arise. One is taking the job specification too literally; the following example sounds unbelievable, but it is true:

Martin was senior chemist at a major cosmetics company. The company was expanding and needed to add a research chemist to the staff. Part of the job specification called for a doctorate in chemistry or molecular biology and at least four years of relevant experience in the cosmetics industry. Several candidates were interviewed by a committee, and finally they narrowed it down to two candidates. Both had doctorate degrees, so the committee looked at other requirements to make a selection. One had excellent credentials, a cooperative and enthusiastic personality but only four- and one-half years of relevant experience. The other candidate was very reserved but had seven years of experience in the field. The committee recommended the second candidate, because he had more experience, even though no one was impressed with the way he conducted himself. Martin was responsible for the hire, but he let the committee "vote," and submitted the second, more experienced, but less personable candidate, as the selection. He was hired and started work two weeks later.

He did not interact well with the others in the lab and became defensive very easily. By the second week, his co-workers realized he was eating chemicals, many of which were not edible. He was summarily terminated, and Martin then recommended that the second candidate be offered the job. She accepted and has been with the company successfully for many years.

The problem Martin made in this hire was that he allowed the selection to be made solely on quantitative items from the job specification. The committee that was supposed to recommend, ended up voting and picking what was probably an obviously bad candidate, because the "numbers" added up to more. Remember, the job specification is only a best guess profile, and you need to use some common sense and good judgment when applying it.

The selection of candidates to interview is also important. In a perfect world, the supervisor of the open position will review all applications and select those that best look like they will be a good fit for the job. In actuality, many personnel departments do an initial screening review and then pass along those candidates selected as the best fit to the supervisor. The quality of this "short list" varies by the ability of the person who did it. Often the initial screening is delegated to a personnel department clerk who does not really understand the job requirements, and you can eliminate good potential employees by having unknowledgeable people doing pre-screening. In the case of our above hypothetical bookkeeper job description, the knowledge of Peachtree Accounting software was a job requirement. An inexperienced screener would probably eliminate every resume that did not say "Peachtree," even if some of those resumes mentioned years of experience on "Sage 50," which is a more advanced version of Peachtree. The best candidates would have been eliminated, simply because not enough attention was given to screening, and you, the supervisor, never would have known about those candidates. If possible, ask to see the resumes of those who were eliminated, to look for mistakes like this.

HIRING

As a supervisor you are likely to be asked to provide input into hiring new employees. This is your opportunity to bring good, qualified people into your organization and it is worthwhile for you to put good effort into helping with the selection. Once the organization has created the job description and job specification, they take the following steps:

Job Announcement. This is a combination of the job description and job specification and is basically an advertisement for the position. These are usually produced by the personnel department, but in smaller companies a supervisor or manager may have to create the job announcement. The important element is accuracy. You need to attract people who will be able to do the work and to do that you must let them know what you want. You also want to promote your company as a good place to work so you should include information about the benefits, working conditions and possibly salary range.

Advertising. Most jobs are advertised in several ways. Online job boards are very common, but don't forget the other ways to reach potential candidates like industry or career specific forums, such as found on LinkedIn. Your current employees should be aware of the opening because many good new employees are recruited by the existing workforce.

Selection. After a period, the applicants are reviewed and a "short list" of interviews is created. These people are called, and an initial interview is scheduled. Some organizations have only the supervisor interview, while others may interview with several people in the organization serially or at once with an interview committee selected to interview the candidates and give an opinion. Some organizations will conduct two, or even three, interviews before making a final selection.

Keep in mind that only the organization hires and fires, so anything a supervisor or committee decides can never be more than a recommendation. When conducting an interview, it is a good idea to ask questions that the applicant will have to answer in depth. Avoid questions with a "yes" or "no" response. The purpose of the interview is twofold; you want to verify a level of knowledge and experience and you, most importantly, want to judge their personality, enthusiasm and ability to work with others. Remember, at this stage you are looking for things that cannot be learned from just reading a resume or application. It is best if you compile a list of interview questions and topics beforehand and then try to consistently ask the same things of each applicant.

Before interviewing, you need to get some guidelines from personnel as to what you can and cannot say. Do not ask any questions regarding, or that could be interpreted as inquiring about race, religion, age, childcare or sexual preference. This can be confusing and becomes somewhat convoluted; For example, you can ask a candidate when they graduated from college, but you cannot ask when they graduated from high school. The logic is that you should not consider age in hiring, and when a person graduated from college is not an exact indication of age, while high school graduation is. Childcare is another sensitive area. Single parents, in the eyes of the government, have the right to equal access to employment. So, if you have a job candidate with a young child, you cannot ask him, "Will you be able to get childcare for your kid?", but you can ask him, "Will you be able to get to work every day?" The list goes on and on, and since you represent your organization, it is important that you know what the limits of conducting an interview are.

Background Check There are two areas of background

checking; former employers and criminal records. The company should check both. If you are asked to check former employment references, use the information from the application to make the calls. Most large former employers will not give out any information besides the dates worked, and whether that person is eligible for re-hire. That doesn't give you a lot to go on, so, if possible, try to talk to former supervisors or co-workers. Generally, if a person has been successful, you will get a good report. If they did not do well people will not say much. You will rarely get a "bad" report, and a "neutral" one is generally a negative indicator. Be careful about checking references from a candidate's current employer. Do not do so without first getting their permission.

Background checks for criminal history vary by state, and there are a lot of do's and don'ts by state. These are usually conducted by an outside vendor who specializes in doing this. They look for criminal records and arrests and verify social security numbers. In some states, you need to let the candidate know that there will be a background check and get a signature (usually on the application) letting you do this. You will find that a surprising number of people have a criminal history which they try to conceal. Most organizations use judgment in hiring a person with a criminal past and an arrest or conviction is not automatic disqualification.

Job Offer and Acceptance – The selected candidate is made an offer, usually by telephone. They may accept immediately, or there may be some negotiation. If an agreement is reached, the offer is normally followed up with a written confirmation which states all the important elements regarding the job, including salary, benefits, working hours, etc., to ensure there is no misunderstanding.

Firing Just like hiring, firing an employee you supervise is done on behalf of the company. We will discuss the process leading up to a termination later in this book, but for now we need to address the actual process of firing after the decision has been reached. Like interviewing, it is something you do not want to approach without help from personnel, but the general principle is, do it quickly. There is no way to make termination fun, for either the person who is being terminated, or the supervisor doing it. Tell them they are terminated, get their keys, or laptop, or whatever it is you need to get back, give them their final paycheck, and escort them out of the building. This is probably the worst part of supervision, and there is nothing you can do to make it feel good. Do not try to smooth it over by telling them that there is probably a better future out there, or that you feel bad for them. These are only things you say to make yourself feel better about what is happening. Do not let them hang around and say goodbye to friends. If they have to do something like clean out their desk, stay with them while they do it. At times like this, you really earn the extra money you make as a supervisor.

Key Concepts

A Job Description describes the work the organization needs done.

A Job Specification is a best guess profile of to be able to do the work in the job description.

Things Your Mother Never Told You

Do not take a job specification too literally.

Be careful of hiring people based solely upon numbers in the job specification.

Assignment

Read your job description and job specification.

How closely do they match what you do and your qualifications at hire?

YOUR GOVERNMENT PARTNER

States, the Federal government, and common law, are all your partners in the workplace. To many people new to supervision and management this seems wrong. We like to think that, as a society, we are unique individuals who are very independent, and many of us have an adverse impression of unrequested government regulation. Actually, government and established customs in employment goes back for a long ways and understanding where it came from can help us understand how we must relate to it.

As a supervisor, everything you do can be interpreted as being done in the name of the organization you work for. Because of this, you need to have some awareness of the employer, government, employee relationship. This is a complex subject, and it is not possible to go into it in detail here, but some historical background will give you a good feeling for the basis of the relationship and the foundation of the laws that govern employment. We will not go into detail on specific laws and issues, which would be enough topic for several books.

The relationship of employment begins over a thousand years ago in Europe. Let's pretend it's the year 1100 and we live in a feudal society. Our little fiefdom is the Duchy of San Carlos, and next to us is the Duchy of Redwood City.

Each one has about 1000 people governed by a Duke and most everyone else in each Duchy is a serf who can't leave, works four days a week farming for the Duke and three days each week farming for themselves. This is a pretty bleak life.

One day, some serfs in the Duchy of San Carlos notice that most of their chickens have been stolen. They get the sheriff who follows a trail of feathers to the Duchy of Redwood City, and finds a group of Redwood City serfs having a chicken Bar-b-Que. They are the chicken thieves, caught greasy handed. Now, do they get arrested and have to make restitution? Nope, the first thing that happens is that the serfs, whose chickens were stolen, go to the Duke of Redwood City and ask him for payment for the chickens his serfs stole! He has responsibility for the actions, and consequences of those actions, of his serfs.

If your knowledge of the Middle Ages is afternoon TV, you probably never realized this. The relationship between the lord and the serfs was actually one of mutual obligation. The noble was responsible for caring for the serfs, and serfs were responsible for supporting the noble. It wasn't quite the single sided relationship we are used to seeing on TV. This was a two-way street, although admittedly one side had things a lot better than the other.

This same type of mutual obligation has been carried into the present, and in a modified sense, the "Lord" is now the employer, and the "serfs" are now the employees. We should not apply this too literally, but it does give us the basis of the relationship. Fast forward a few more centuries, and we can see this transitioning into formal employment responsibility:

It's Dodge City, Kansas in the 1800's. This is a wild town with gunfights and gamblers and mud streets and, important to us, both a seamstress and an old time Telegraph

Company office. Back in these distant days, accurate time was "high tech" and having a watch was like having a satellite cellphone. Many shop owners displayed large clocks in their place of business to attract customers, who came in to set their watches or just to know the time if they didn't have a watch. Besides telegrams the Telegraph Company leased clocks to local merchants and part of the lease was a service agreement to keep the clock running.

The Dodge City Seamstress had clock in her seamstress shop, and the clock had stopped ticking. She sent her assistant to the Telegraph Company office several times to inform them that the clock was broken and needed to be fixed. No one came to fix the clock. Finally, on a Friday afternoon she whipped herself into a frenzy over the fact that the clock was broken, and stomped out of the seamstress shop, through the muddy streets lined with saloons and horse droppings and burst, with anger fired righteousness, into the Telegraph Company office. "I demand! she yelled, "that you fix my clock!"

Only it was Friday afternoon in Dodge City and the staff and cronies hanging around the Telegraph Company office were drunk, very drunk. The manager of the office staggered over to the counter, tried to reach over the top, (it later came out in the trial that his arms were not long enough to actually reach over the top since he was so short,) and while clasping and unclasping his little fingers, he said in his most lecherous voice, "Come on over here honey and I'll fix your clock!" before sliding off the back the back side of the counter and onto the floor.

Our now super enraged seamstress, stomped back out of the office, back down the street to her attorney's office and began the process of filing a lawsuit. Whom did she sue? Not the creepy little drunk guy, he had no real money. She sued his employer, the Telegraph Company, for inflicting emotional distress, and she won, and they paid, just like the duke whose serfs stole the chickens and got caught. It is interesting to note that the little guy who reached over the counter and made lecherous remarks, did not even testify at the trial, was too drunk to do anything except fall over, and finally, the seamstress who was well over six feet tall could have easily beaten him to a pulp. This case somehow stuck in everyone's memory, as it will probably now stick in yours, and it is the beginning of, *"Respondeat Superior"* in our legal system, which basically means, "Let the master answer", in Latin.

That still applies, and in general, anything you do or say can reflect back upon your employer, as long as it was even remotely in the course of your employment. So, if you ask a job candidate why he is bothering to look for a job at age 60, or if you tell the cute secretary upstairs that you wish she would give you a kiss, you are doing these things in the name of your employer, just like the serfs who stole the chickens or the little drunk guy who tried to grab at the seamstress.

There are basically three classifications of laws that govern your actions in the workplace. These are Federal law, State law and finally common law, which are those laws which exist by custom (most of common law is codified into state laws by definition.) It could take a lifetime to review this confusing roster of laws and court decisions, so we won't attempt to do it here. Federal law applies everywhere, and state laws are a checkerboard of different things applying in different locations. All you need to succeed in the workplace is enough knowledge to have an awareness of when you could be approaching an area that is highly regulated. This way, you will know when to seek more knowledge, or personnel department assistance, before proceeding. Let's look at the two areas, discrimination, and harassment, that a supervisor has to be most aware of:

Discrimination This is the one you hear about most and it seems to always be in the news.

The basis for discrimination rules is the concept that all people have a right to be treated equally in the workplace and other economic pursuits. After all, each of us has the obligation to pay taxes, obey the laws, and many of us to get drafted into the military, so it follows that if we suffer the detriments of being part of a society, we ought to have the right to participate on equal footing for the benefits of that society. To be discriminated against under the law, a person must be part of what is called a "protected class," which means there is a law passed specifically to protect a person falling into that category. The common protected classes are:

Sex
Sexual Preference
Race
Pregnancy
Disability (including HIV)
Age
Military Service
Bankruptcy
Genetics
Citizenship.

To discriminate you basically treat one class of people (see above) differently than the others in the workplace. If you never hire old people because their company paid health insurance costs more, you are discriminating. If you never promote Christians because you don't like their God, then you are discriminating. If you always recommend women for a smaller raise than men -- because their husbands work, and they don't really need the money anyhow-- you are discriminating. If you do not hire or promote females to certain jobs because they get pregnant and quit, or take lots of time off, then you are discriminating. It is important to remember that how you feel or what you think has nothing to do with discrimination. It is what you do, or do not do, that counts, and it counts against your employer.

Harassment This one is best thought of as, "Creating a Hostile Environment" which is designed to make a person quit or just make them miserable. Think of the words "oppressive and intimidating atmosphere" when trying to understand harassment. People who are harassed can (and usually do) fit under one of the protected classes, but they do not have to. Harassment cases can take many unforeseen twists and here is a recent case from a western state:

Emily worked as the Senior Administrative Aide to the president of a large organization. She reported to the office manager, but most all of her interface was with the president. The president was a woman who was openly gay. She gave Emily some small gifts and showed an interest in her that could have been interpreted as going beyond just a working interest, but over the period of about one year the relationship never turned into anything else, although the somewhat mutual interest and flirting continued.

The office manager, to whom Emily reported, did enter into a personal, out of the office, relationship with the President and, apparently seeing Emily as a rival, the office manager did her best to make Emily's life miserable. Her actions included extreme criticism of Emily's performance, arbitrary hour changes, belittling her in front of other employees, impossible assignments and a host of other words and deeds designed to make Emily quit or transfer out of the department. Her job performance reviews suddenly fell from, "Excellent" to "Does not meet standards".

Emily retained an attorney and for a year kept a secret journal of all the things her supervisor, the office manager, did and said to her. On the advice of her attorney, she also began seeing a doctor for treatment of her work related stress. After gathering evidence for a year, Emily sued her employer and based upon recommendation from their legal department and their insurer, the company settled without going to trial for approximately $400,000 and gave Emily, who was eligible to retire in three years, an early retirement with full benefits.

Note that this case had nothing to do with sexual harassment. It was about an office manager who created a hostile environment to make an employee quit. It is also interesting to note that the president, who could have easily stopped this by talking to the office manager, did not do so, but after the settlement, the president was not disciplined and continued working for the company as if nothing had happened!

This brings us to the area of employee discipline. It must be fair, and it must be controlled so that a "rogue manager" like the president and office manager noted above, cannot damage the company through their actions. You will also find that employees who are not performing well at their jobs rarely blame themselves, and often try to claim harassment or discrimination rather than face up to the fact that they are not doing well at the job. Virtually every large company uses a variation of what is called, "progressive discipline" to make sure that disciplining an employee is done both fairly and in the interests of productivity and harmony. Progressive Discipline and correcting behavior is the subject of our next chapter.

Key Concepts

Discrimination is an action against someone in a protected

class.

Harassment is an accumulation of acts designed to make someone miserable.

Things Your Mother Never Told You

If someone complains to you of discrimination, harassment or sexual harassment go to your   supervisor and personnel department immediately. Do not ignore complaints.

Be careful of people who want to, "only tell you" And will not make statements to others.

Assignment

What is your company's policy on sexual harassment?

PROGRESSIVE DISCIPLINE

Most employers who need to correct the behavior of employees use a system called "progressive discipline." Progressive discipline starts with an informal conversation and can end several steps later with termination. The purpose of progressive discipline is to let the employee formally know what they are doing, or not doing, and give them the opportunity to correct the inappropriate behavior(s). The use of progressive discipline is recognized by the courts as an impartial method of modifying behavior. If your company is involved in litigation because of an employee termination, having used progressive discipline can help show responsible behavior on the part of the organization.

Organizations are concerned about how the behavior of employees is addressed. An employee is an asset, and if things are not going well, it is generally worth the effort to try to get the employee "back on track" rather than simply replace them. Beyond that, the company needs to protect itself from litigation and accusations from employees who are terminated. Sometimes an employee who is terminated does not want to address the possibility that they really did not do well at the job and will convince themselves that they are really being discriminated against as members of a protected class or are being harassed. If there is a standard, consistent, monitored and controlled method of addressing unsatisfactory performance, the company has a lot better protection against false accusations. And finally, progressive discipline is a check upon the supervisor, to make sure that the behavior change requested is realistic and legitimate, and actually in accordance with company policy.

The first, and most important, thing you need to know about progressive discipline is that it is NOT punishment; it is a method of correcting employee behavior, and it is not designed to make them feel bad or guilty, and it is not a stigma that stays with them once the issue is resolved. Once the correct behavior is achieved, the matter is finished and forgotten, unless the problem occurs again. There are five basic steps of progressive discipline:

Informal verbal warning
Formal verbal warning
Written warning
Suspension without pay for up to three days.
Termination

There is some variation to the steps of progressive discipline. These include two formal verbal warnings or two written warnings, or some may involve sessions with a committee of management and workers, while some may mandate meetings with a union representative. You should find out what the specific features of the system are in your company before beginning any discipline.

At each stage in the process except termination, the employee should be told the following:

What is wrong
Why it is wrong
What, should be, or should have been, done (What must be done to correct)
What will happen if it is not corrected (The next step in the disciplinary process)
When the employee's performance will be reviewed for compliance.

Discipline is normally done in steps. Each step should be documented either by a note to the employee's file, and/or a copy of documents given to the employee. The most important element is a follow up meeting (usually two to four weeks) at a specific time and place to discuss improvement of behavior. Without the follow up, the process does not work very well. Be careful when conducting a disciplinary session that you do not adopt demeanor which infers that you think the employee is stupid, or inferior, or "bad". Such behavior on the part of the supervisor only increases the conflict and makes the process more difficult. The best way to approach it is to realize that you both work for the same company, and this meeting or action is to put the employee on the correct track for success with the organization.

Before beginning progressive discipline, have an informal, but direct, conversation with the employee telling them what it is wrong and why is wrong and what needs to be done to correct it. This will correct about 90% of your employee problems.

The following is a typical "written warning" in the progressive discipline process:

10/20/2019

Dear Joe:

On 10/6/2019, we discussed that you are not getting the contract periodic billings out on time. There have been several instances over the last few months where the submission dates for progress billings have been missed, causing our payment requests to be deferred to the next month by the customer. Since our last conversation on 10/6/2019, you submitted the payment requests for Murphy's Shipping and Megadeath Rocket Company late, causing over $430,000 in billing to be deferred for 30 days by the customers. We need these payment requests submitted properly and on time. You were supposed to build a tickler file from the documents on each project, note the due dates and have the requests in on time. Failure to do so delays payments and gives us cash flow problems.

You are required to make a complete and accurate tickler file of the dates and submit the payment requests on time.

We will review your performance again on 11/4/2014, at 10AM in your office. If the billings have not been processed correctly, the next step in the disciplinary process will be suspension for three days without pay. You need to know that if the billing problem is not corrected this disciplinary process may ultimately result in termination.

Sincerely,

Supervisor

This letter is a generic sample, and before beginning any action beyond an informal warning, you should discuss the situation with your supervisor and/or the personnel department. There are a few things to keep in mind when disciplining an employee:

1) There may be a good reason why they are not doing it right. Often the beginning of the discipline procedure brings out problems with work organization, priorities, or instructions, which make it difficult or impossible for an employee to do their job correctly.

2) You may be asking for an arbitrary standard, or the expectation you are setting is not realistic. Be sure the goal for the employee is a realistic one and is sanctioned by the company.

3) The required behavior is part of the employee's job and they have been formally told this.

In extreme cases such as fighting, theft or other serious actions, the process is usually abridged to move right to termination or suspension. As a supervisor, you should keep in communication with both your supervisor and the personnel department, to make sure you understand, and follow, the specific procedures in place in the organization in which you work.

Key Concepts

Progressive discipline is never punishment.

The beginning of progressive discipline will often reveal workplace problems that make work difficult for an employee.

Things Your Mother Never Told You

The same people who tell you to, "Fire that guy" may not back you up at the final stage.

Everyone who works for you should always know how they are doing.

Assignment

What is your company's policy on sexual harassment?

THE FUTURE

You now know a lot about supervision - more than most supervisors who have been doing it for years. Use this knowledge as a beginning and make your workplace your laboratory. Learn from what you see happening around you, and discover what works, and does not work, in your unique situation. Remember that supervision is always in a state of flux and ambiguity. Living with this is part of your role as a supervisor.